SPIRITUAL TRANSMISSION

SPIRITUAL TRANSMISSION

*Paradoxes and Dilemmas
on the Spiritual Path*

AMIR FREIMANN

*Foreword by Paul Cohen
Afterword by Ken Wilber*

MONKFISH BOOK PUBLISHING COMPANY
RHINEBECK, NEW YORK

Paperback ISBN: 978-1-939681-95-9
eBook ISBN: 978-1-939681-96-6

Library of Congress Cataloging-in-Publication Data

Names: Freimann, Amir, 1958- author.
Title: Spiritual transmission : paradoxes and dilemmas on the spiritual path
  / Amir Freimann ; foreword by Paul Cohen ; afterword by Ken Wilbur.
Description: Rhinebeck, New York : Monkfish Book Publishing Company, 2018. |
  Includes bibliographical references.
Identifiers: LCCN 2018030578 (print) | LCCN 2018046244 (ebook) | ISBN
  9781939681966 (eBook) | ISBN 9781939681959 (pbk. : alk. paper)
Subjects: LCSH: Spiritual life. | Religious adherents. | Religious leaders. |
  Interpersonal relations--Religious aspects.
Classification: LCC BL624 (ebook) | LCC BL624 .F743 2018 (print) | DDC
  204--dc23
LC record available at https://lccn.loc.gov/2018030578

Book and cover design by Colin Rolfe

Monkfish Book Publishing Company
22 East Market Street, Suite 304
Rhinebeck, New York 12572
U.S.A.
(845) 876-4861
monkfishpublishing.com

Dedicated to all my teachers and students—
past, present and future

TABLE OF CONTENTS

FOREWORD

S piritual transmission is the deeply personal mechanism that enlivens and empowers the relationship between spiritual teachers and students; as such, it is one of the most important aspects of the spiritual path. And yet it is also one of the most overlooked subjects of contemporary spiritual literature. When I say overlooked, I mean that objective treatments of the subject are rare. There are indeed many books that espouse the need for such relationships, but in the main, they are sectarian in nature, coming from specific traditions and recommending specific gurus and teachings.

Part of the subject's importance lies in the sheer numbers of people whose lives have been impacted powerfully by such relationships. Starting in the 1960s, the West experienced an explosion of spiritual teachers and teachings, coming primarily from the East which was complemented by a groundswell of development in Western teachings and teachers borrowing heavily from Eastern religions. As far as I know, there has never been a scientific study attempting to quantify just how many people became involved in spiritual teachings of this ilk. But, based on the sheer number of spiritual teachers and the fact that many of them have had thousands of students, there is good reason to believe that they have numbered in the millions.

Relationships between students and their spiritual teachers were, and are, by and large, lifelong relationships. Once forged, they are difficult to break completely. Ask students of spiritual teachers just how significant those relationships are to them, and more often than not, you will hear that their relationship to their teacher is the most important and primary relationship in their life. And yet, in hindsight, it's become apparent that many of the relationships that flourished in the 1960s and beyond wound up ending badly, often mired in controversy over issues of abuse of power.

My own life was similarly impacted. I became a devoted spiritual seeker during my first year in college. I read voluminously on the subject and went to see and listen to every spiritual teacher I could find. Spiritual seeking became the pivot around which the rest of my life revolved. I came to believe that spiritual enlightenment and liberation was the answer of answers—that *all* of the many forms of suffering from which I desperately wished to escape could be alleviated with the attainment of this singular goal. Indeed, that seemed to be the promise of such teachings—at least to my young mind.

At the age of twenty-two, I married an emotionally unbalanced woman. I thought I could help her—particularly through the spiritual teachings in which I was then immersed. She became increasingly mentally ill and refused all psychotherapy, believing it to be inferior and even adverse to spiritual teachings. She herself became intensely involved with the teaching that only love was real, and that the material world in which we lived was an illusion based on our refusal to love unconditionally. This belief, combined with her illness, which was later diagnosed as borderline personality disorder exacerbated by alcoholism, created suffering upon suffering for both of us. And yet, the more deeply she sank into her illness, the more strongly I held to my belief that the answer lay in spiritual attainment.

Because of her belief in the unreality of the material world, my wife increasingly refrained from gainful employment. In this way, she became ever more dependent upon me for the basic demands of life. So while her illness in many ways deepened my commitment to the spiritual path, it also limited my ability to make the kind of commitments often called for in spiritual life. At the same time, I began to fear for her life if I were to divorce her. Suicide had entered our lexicon. I felt stuck on the horns of a moral dilemma that I lacked the wherewithal to resolve by myself. What kept me going for many years were the spiritual experiences often delivered at the hands of powerful teachers. And yet, I couldn't help but notice that while these experiences helped me to cope with a difficult marriage, they seemed unable to touch the deeper roots of the suffering in which my wife and I were trapped.

My last teacher was Andrew Cohen. I met him in 1993 while on a bookselling trip to Portland, Oregon. He was a compelling teacher. Not only was he able to transmit higher states of awareness (simply by talking), but he was also surrounded by highly intelligent students from all around the world, many of whom had given up their previous lives, marriages and careers to be with him. What became apparent over a period of time was that the real action was to be found by living in his community, which would have meant leaving my wife, since she was unwilling to devote herself to Andrew's teaching in that way. Eventually we worked out an arrangement whereby we were living separately, and so, slowly but surely, I was able to make my way into the communal living that had become the still unpublished cornerstone of Andrew's teaching.

By 1999, I was living in a communal house near Boston, where Andrew had opened a new center. But aspects of communal living began to grate on me. I came to feel that we students, and our "enlightenment," were secondary to what I perceived as "empire building" by Andrew. I was disturbed by the amount of labor we were required to put into the new center, all of which was unpaid, and I was distressed by the way many of the students mimicked the way Andrew talked and dressed. This struck me as a sign of immaturity and proof of the absence of independent thought, which seemed inimical to spiritual enlightenment as I had come to understand it.

A few months in, I came down with the flu and stayed in bed for about a week recovering. During that time, I read Mariana Caplan's first edition of *Halfway Up the Mountain: The Error of Premature Claims to Enlightenment*. Even though Andrew Cohen was put forth in the book as an exemplar of someone who had "gone all the way," the book brought to the surface many of the doubts that had been brewing within me. So I wrote Andrew a letter expressing my doubts, hoping that he would address them directly. Instead, he had a senior student phone me at the house where I was living to deliver a message over the loudspeaker so that my housemates could hear what was said. The gist of the message was that my doubts were an expression of ego, and that I could either get with the program and put those doubts aside, or leave—that very night. I felt viscerally that my ego was on the chopping block, so to speak, but I also couldn't help but feel that were my ego to be decimated it would simply be replaced by an even bigger ego—Andrew's. I decided to keep my own ego intact and, indeed, left that night, explaining to my housemates that I couldn't abide by a spiritual system that didn't allow for doubts.

Leaving a spiritual teacher and teaching is a painful thing to do, perhaps even more so when the student has been abused in some way by the teacher. In the case of Andrew's community, I had seen that when other students left, they often became an object of scorn for Andrew and the other students. But the real pain comes from the fact that once a spiritual teaching is deeply absorbed by the student, it becomes the filter through which the student understands their life experience. Sans the interpretive filter of the teaching, you no longer have a way to make sense of your experience. What becomes necessary is some new way to parse your experience with the teaching and the teacher—and your own life.

For me, that new way came via the editing of a book submitted to my then-new book publishing company from a former student of Andrew's—André van der Braak, who had written a memoir of his years as Andrew's student. André's book became *Enlightenment Blues: My Years with an American Guru*. This was André's first book, and it was written in his second language, since he is Dutch, so the editorial process went on for months, during which time I not only had the opportunity to straighten out some of André's English, but my own mind as well. What we (or at least I in my editing) aimed for with the book was to deliver a homeopathic dose of anger to other struggling students of Andrew Cohen—just enough to liberate them, but not so much as to put them off the spiritual path altogether.

While working on *Enlightenment Blues*, I began to research widely into other spiritual communities with prominent and charismatic teachers or gurus and to find out what had happened to students who left. There were a lot of them! Many of these former students had established online groups where they could support each other; explore what had happened to them. I became aware of how endemic this kind of spiritual circumstance was—and yet, within the field of spiritual literature, it was only described in either personal spiritual memoirs or frankly negative treatises on gurus, the best known of which at that time was Joel Kramer and Diana Alstad's *The Guru Papers: Masks of Authoritarian Power*.

Some thirteen years passed between my publishing of *Enlightenment Blues* and Amir Friemann approaching me with the manuscript that you now hold in your hands, *Spiritual Transmission*. What is notable about Amir is that even though he also went through a painful breakup with his own spiritual teacher—also Andrew Cohen—he never soured on the notion and necessity of the spiritual guru. Indeed, he doesn't seem to have soured on Andrew. Instead, Amir recognizes and focuses on the genuine need for spiritual transmission by awakened teachers, which he sets out to better understand by spending countless hours interviewing spiritual teachers *and* their students. Amir brings a truly open mind and considerable skill as an interviewer to some of the most significant spiritual questions—and teachers—of our time.

Spiritual Transmission contains never-before-published interviews with well-known spiritual teachers and thinkers, which are enhanced by the reflections of their own students, as well as by Amir's own extensive experience as a student and seeker. He refrains from hasty conclusions, sometimes to the point where I questioned (to myself) whether he valued the question over the answer. But if, at times, that frustrated me as an editor/publisher who wanted to make a *book*, Amir always struck me as a devoted journalist of the spirit. While I feel sure this book will not contain his last thoughts on the subject, I do consider it a definitive work on the subject, due in no small measure to Ken Wilber's extraordinary afterword which contains the seeds of a new understanding of spiritual transmission that is sorely needed today. Through the combination of Amir's thoughts and interviews and Ken Wilber's afterword, I have come to a better understanding of the trajectory of my own life, particularly the limits, as well as the promise, of the spiritual relationship to the guru, and why gurus—and our own lives with them—so often go astray. It is my hope that you, the reader, like me, will find useful guidance here.

—PAUL COHEN
PUBLISHER, MONKFISH BOOK PUBLISHING COMPANY
RHINEBECK, NEW YORK
JUNE 2018

In the past, we have viewed expert and ignorant in whatever sphere—teacher and student, priest and supplicant, coach and athlete, parent and child—as discrete entities with a specific causal relationship. Experts were active and powerful—their task to lead; their polar components, non-experts, filled a passive role—their task to follow. I would suggest that the truth has always been larger and more interesting than this. But we couldn't know it, for it would have made reality too big, greater than our capacity to handle it.

—CHARLES M. JOHNSTON, *NECESSARY WISDOM: MEETING THE CHALLENGE OF A NEW CULTURAL MATURITY*

THE WHAT, WHY AND HOW
OF THIS BOOK

Nearly seven years after I broke off my twenty-one-year relationship with spiritual teacher Andrew Cohen—by far the most significant, intense, challenging and rewarding relationship of my adult life—I decided to create this book. It has since taken me hundreds of hours of interviews with teachers and students, who helped me cast light on the spiritual teacher-student relationship; that was followed by perhaps thousands of hours of reading, editing, contemplation and writing. I'm pleased to present you with my findings, humble though they may be, regarding the paradoxical nature of that relationship. I write in the hope that we, students and teachers alike, can begin to come to better grips with the meaning of our relationship with each other.

The interviews and stories you are about to read are deeply personal in nature. Such is the subject matter itself. The questions I have sought to elucidate in this book are the very ones that I myself have struggled with all these years.

JULY 1987
JERUSALEM

In the summer of 1987, I was twenty-nine years old, finishing up my fifth year of medical studies at the Hadassah Medical School and my fourth year of Chinese medicine studies at a private school. And I was in total turmoil about my life. The turmoil had to do with Andrew Cohen.

He was an ordinary-looking Jewish-American kid from New York, which is how I fondly thought of him, even though he was only three years my elder. My experience of sitting every evening with Andrew and a small group of people in a friend's living room in Jerusalem— listening to him answer people's questions about enlightenment, liberation, timelessness and the absolute reality with utter simplicity and directness, as well as having my own personal revelatory conversations with him—was catalyzing a tectonic shift in me.

I had caught the bug of seeking spiritual liberation when I was sixteen, but I had always been suspicious and even hostile toward the idea of becoming the student of any spiritual teacher. That seemed to me a sure recipe for spiritual slavery—the very opposite of what I was looking for. Although I had lived for two years with a delightfully free-spirited Zen master in Japan, who I spoke of as my teacher, and I intended to go back to meditate with him after I completed my studies, I never considered him as my *Teacher*. But there I was, contemplating the possibility that in Andrew I had met my *Teacher*, and it was driving me crazy. How could I know if he was my true *Teacher*? How could anyone know? What did *Teacher* even mean?

On a warm July morning, the upheaval I was experiencing grew so intense that once I arrived at the hospital, I couldn't imagine joining my team at the surgery department. We were to study anesthesia that day. But I needed to figure out my relationship with Andrew first, I told myself, and without further delay. My life depended on it. But how could I know? My mind seemed completely useless in the face of my questions. I walked back and forth on the hospital lawn in an agitated state for what felt like hours. Then, in despair I thought: I should try to have a nap; maybe the answer would come to me in my sleep. I lay down under a tree, but the heat, the flies and my agitation made it a hopeless attempt. "I give up," I thought. "I might as well join my team and use the rest of the day for studying." I started to get up, but just as I was halfway to standing I was catapulted into a state of unitive consciousness.

I have no idea how long I was in that state, for I had no perception of "I" nor of time. It seems to me that if somebody had been standing next to me with a stopwatch, they would have measured only a few seconds, but I was in a "dimension" or an "existential state" in which a fraction of a second and eternity are one and the same. I cannot use the words "experience" or "knowing" for it, because "experience" and "knowing" require a split between the knower (the subject, "I") and the known (the object of experience or knowing), and in the state I experienced that day outside the hospital in Jerusalem, there was no such split.

In that fraction of a second, the very foundation of my being seemed to shift. When I found myself back in the world of self and time, I knew that Andrew had always been and would always be my Teacher, and that somehow I had always known that.

I stumbled to the phone booth at the hospital entrance and called the house where Andrew was staying.

"Hello," he answered in his now familiar voice.

"Andrew?" I said, "This is Andrew. I mean, hi, Andrew, this is Amir." I couldn't think straight.

"I'm yours," I said.

I could feel Andrew smiling on the other end.

"I knew that since we first met," he replied. "Why don't you come over and tell me what happened?"

SEPTEMBER 15, 1987
TOTNES, UNITED KINGDOM

A few days after completing my end-of-year exams in medical school I flew over to the U.K., and was warmly welcomed into one of the *sangha* (Sanskrit for community) houses of Andrew's students in Totnes, a town in England's picturesque South Devon region, where Andrew was staying.

A few weeks after arriving in Totnes, I spent one evening after *satsang* (Sanskrit for being in the company of a guru) with Andrew and the people who were living with him. The next day I received a message from him that he wanted to talk with me, so I went over to his house. As we sat together in the living room, Andrew laid out for me the full picture of my psycho-spiritual makeup. He said that on the one hand, he found me an exceptionally warm, trusting, serious and committed man, and felt a deep connection with me; but on the other hand, he felt a heavy presence of ego in me, and he and the other people with him had been very aware of it during our meeting the night before. He said it was rare to have these two extremes co-existing in the same person. Then he said: "You want to become as light as a feather, and this may take a few years. I suggest that you forget any plans you may have other than being with me. Think of yourself as a wandering monk. This means you should completely forget about your medical career."

That was a lot to let in, and Andrew saw that and got up to make coffee for both of us. During the few minutes that he was in the kitchen, I decided I was going to follow his advice. Instantly, I experienced a change in my attitude. When he came back, holding two cups of cappuccino, I told him: "Andrew, something completely unexpected has just happened to me. Only a few minutes ago I was dreading the possibility that you would suggest that I completely discard my medical career, and now I feel like I've just dropped a few sandbags, to help my takeoff."

And so it happened that I ultimately and irrevocably discarded my plans to become a medical doctor, and never looked back.

But my meeting with Andrew that day also marked another significant turning point in my life. Until that day I had never liked coffee, and under any other circumstances I would have refused it, but when your guru makes you a cup of cappuccino, you drink it. I drank it—and to my utter surprise, I loved it. That day I became a coffee lover.

NOVEMBER 1990
SANTA CRUZ AND MILL VALLEY, CALIFORNIA

In mid-1988 I moved, together with Andrew and over one-hundred of his European students, to live in the United States. We lived for about a year in Boston and then moved to Marin County, California.

At about the middle of 1990 the pressure on me by Andrew and my friends in the community, to face my "Israeli macho" conditioning, was becoming unbearable for me. I could see some of what they were pointing out to me, but I also felt that there wasn't much I could do about it. I fell into despair and considered giving up my spiritual aspirations and returning to "life in the world." At some point I left the community and moved to Santa Cruz, a few hours away from where the community was living. I rented a room in a house there and spent a few months working and thinking about what I wanted to do with my life. The crisis ended surprisingly with a dream.

In my dream I was sitting face to face with Andrew, close to him, telling him in great detail all I was seeing and understanding about my psychological and spiritual condition, all the obstacles I saw in my way, which of them I had already faced, which of them I felt I could overcome and which of them I had no confidence that I could overcome. Andrew listened to me very attentively without responding, and when I finished speaking (in the dream it was after a long time), he said to me very simply: "It all depends on what you want."

I woke up immediately. It was still completely dark outside. The dream was so lucid, so tangible, that it could have been real. I knew that in the dream I was clearer and more accurate than I could ever be when I was awake, and I decided to write down all I had told Andrew in the dream while it was still fresh in my memory. I opened my diary and began writing feverishly. I wrote about the obstacles in my way, but as I read what I wrote I *knew* these particular obstacles could not stop me. At the end of the process I had all the obstacles clearly laid out on the pages of my diary, and none of them was a real obstacle. I knew what I wanted.

At 9:00 a.m. I called the office of the community and asked to give Andrew the message that I wanted to come back. Minutes later I received a call from Andrew. I told him what had happened, and asked him to let me come back to the community. "Why don't you come over and meet with me and a few of your friends," he suggested. A few days later I moved back to the community.

JANUARY 1991
BODHGAYA, INDIA
(DURING A MONTH-LONG RETREAT)

"Andrew, what happens when we die?" The question came from a Bhutanese monk at our month-long retreat; he wore saffron robes, and had been coming regularly to satsang with Andrew.

"I don't know," Andrew said, "I don't have any memory of it. But when I get there, I'll send you a postcard."

We all laughed, and I started thinking: Do I know anything about this question? Is there anything in my experience that could indicate to me what happens after we die? What if I died right now—would everything stop or would something of me continue?

I sat there, imagining that I had died, suddenly, without anything leading to it, and I *knew* that my death would have absolutely no effect on my relationship with Andrew. It wouldn't even register on that level—it would be completely insignificant. I didn't know how I knew that, but I had no doubt that it was true, and as I contemplated it I was flooded with intense ecstasy. I was thinking about death and I was totally ecstatic, because I knew my death would mean nothing for my relationship with Andrew.

JANUARY 1998
RISHIKESH, INDIA
(DURING A MONTH-LONG RETREAT)

"I've just inherited a lot of money and I don't have to work anymore," said the man sitting in front of Andrew in satsang. "On the one hand, I am attracted to do social work and help the needy, and on the other, I am pulled to dedicate my life to the spiritual quest. What should I do?"

"You should find what it is that pulls you like a black hole, that if you immerse yourself in it you will disappear into it, and then you should give yourself wholeheartedly to that," Andrew replied.

I contemplated for a minute what that black hole was for me, and quickly came to the answer: It was the purity and absolute nature of the enlightenment teachings that I felt drawn to and wanted to immerse myself completely in.

I sat there, feeling happy with that answer, until it suddenly hit me that it was my relationship with Andrew himself, much more than his teachings, that I was pulled to. *What? How could that be?* The answer made no sense to me. How could my relationship with Andrew, who is just a human being, be more powerful and all-consuming than spiritual teachings? To my mind, the answer made no sense, but at the same time my heart was exploding with it, and tears were streaming down my face.

I knew I had to ask Andrew what this meant, so after satsang ended, I went and asked to talk with him. "I have a spiritual question I want to ask you," I said, and told him what had happened and my bewilderment about the insight I had had.

"You're right!" Andrew exclaimed when I finished. "Do you know why? First of all, because I *am* the teachings! Secondly, it's also a perfect answer because a smart guy like you can find a way to remain separate and intact in your relationship with the teachings, but you sense and know that you will lose yourself completely in your relationship with me."

JUNE 2006
FOXHOLLOW, MASSACHUSETTS

Foxhollow was the world center of EnlightenNext, the international organization and spiritual community that grew around Andrew, with a dozen centers in Europe, the United Sates, Israel and India. Andrew and sixty to seventy of his students lived at Foxhollow, and the place also functioned as an ashram or monastery where people practiced meditation and various physical practices a few hours each day, as well as engaged in intensive individual and collective enquiry.

One weekend at Foxhollow, the tension became almost palpable. It was a moment of truth for the men among Andrew's oldest students, and I was one of them. After months of intensive practice and countless meetings among us, Andrew felt that the time was ripe for a significant change in our relationship with him and our ability to take more responsibility for the development of the community. A meeting with him was scheduled for the morning of the following day, Saturday. In a message that Andrew sent to all of us, he emphasized that it was important that we be ready for the next step, both all together and individually.

It had become clear to everyone that I was the weak link in the group. My friends were concerned about the effect that my weaknesses—self-doubt, lack of confidence and emotional instability—would have on this important meeting. I promised them that I would do all I could not to disappoint them, but in my heart I was not confident at all that I would keep my promise.

That evening, Andrew played with his jazz band at a club in one of the nearby towns. I drove with a few friends to the gig. As soon as I entered the club, Andrew noticed me, even as he was busy setting up his drum kit, and signaled for me to come over to him. As I leaned toward him, he whispered forcefully: "Amir, tomorrow we are going to have a very important meeting, and its success depends very much on you. But rather than do everything to face your weakness and come prepared to the meeting, you chose to come here, drink beer and enjoy the music. It seems that you don't really care. But I do. A lot. Would you please leave the club for me?"

Shaken and on the verge of tears, I left the club and drove back to Foxhollow. I didn't know what to do. I went to the meditation hall, sat down in the middle of the large, empty space, and meditated through the night. In those hours of meditation, I rediscovered immovable stability, which was not dependent in any way upon me.

In the morning, when we met with Andrew, it was clear to everyone—without exchanging a word—that something had settled down and completely relaxed in me. I shared with everyone what happened.

"Andrew, I don't understand," I said. "I've been meditating for thirty years, but nothing like this has ever happened to me; I've never had such a meditation. What happened?"

"It's very simple," Andrew replied. "You're a narcissist, so even your meditation is for yourself. Last night you meditated for me. That's what made all the difference."

DECEMBER 26, 2008
FOXHOLLOW, MASSACHUSETTS

"We've been putting so much energy, time and money into the Israeli center, but it's never taken off," Andrew said. "So, as disappointing as it is for me and for everybody, we've decided to close it down. I want you to move back to Foxhollow and be part of the core group here."

I sank into my chair, feeling as if all the energy were draining out of my body. The room suddenly turned darker. A horrible feeling of total and final failure came over me. But the failure wasn't just of our Israeli center and of me as its co-leader. At that moment I sensed that, for me, the failure really lay in my relationship with Andrew and the promise it had carried.

In a way, that moment was the culmination of a half-year process, during which my mistrust in Andrew's motivation had grown. I mistrusted his willingness to support me in the independence, strength, creativity and responsibility I was discovering. The stronger and more independent I became, both as a leader and as a cultural activist, the more tension I felt growing between us. Being sent back to Foxhollow also meant that I would be again in Andrew's sphere of tight control, which would be a major setback to my growing autonomy.

From the bottom of my sinkhole, I heard myself mumbling, "I cannot do that. I cannot leave Israel and all the projects I'm involved in. That would be completely wrong."

"Why don't you think about it, and let's talk again tomorrow," Andrew said. "I think it would be good for you to be here, with your brothers and close to me. You've become a leader, and here you'd be part of the worldwide revolution, rather than wasting your time in Israel."

"I cannot leave Israel," I repeated, now with a little more determination. "That would be a total letdown of my friends and colleagues there, and of my own integrity. I'm not going to do that."

As I stepped out of Andrew's office into the freezing wind and began walking back to the house where I was staying during my visit, I already knew that this conversation marked the end of my relationship with Andrew as my Teacher. It was the first time in nearly twenty-two years that I had told him directly that he was wrong and that I wasn't going to obey his instructions. That meant that I trusted myself more than I trusted him. That meant the termination of our teacher-student "contract." But at that moment, for me it also meant failure, disappointment and heartache.

The breakdown of my relationship with Andrew left me with one big, wide open question: *"What was it all about?"* Five years later, when Andrew's worldwide organization of EnlightenNext collapsed, I decided to engage even more fully with that question, and take its exploration as far as I could—at least for myself, at this point in my spiritual process. I didn't know where this would lead or what discoveries I would make in the process, but just the idea of diving into the mystery of the teacher-student relationship made my nerves tingle with excitement.

I started off by reading every book and article on the subject that I could find, and taking my first steps in interviewing teachers and students in Israel. My very first interview was with Peter (Hakim) Young, a British Sufi teacher who was visiting Israel with his Israeli-born wife. On a sunny morning in Tel Aviv, we met in a café on Sheinkin Street, and I vividly remember our first exchange. I asked Hakim to tell me about his relationship with his teacher, Bulent Rauf, and he replied that the man had never regarded himself as a teacher but rather as "a fellow student."

"Gosh," I thought, "this project is going to be trickier than I thought."

My second interviewee was with Aikido teacher Miles Kessler, in another café in Tel Aviv. At the end of the interview, I asked him if he was willing to refer me to a couple of his students to interview, and his response seriously impressed me: "Since you heard from me only good things about myself," he said, "I think you should get a more balanced picture, so I'll introduce you to two former students of mine with whom the relationship did not end well. If they agree to be interviewed, I think you'll get quite a different perspective from them." Indeed, the picture I got from those former students was much more complex and dilemmatic than I got from him.

Israel is a mecca for spiritual teachers, and I went on to interview about a dozen visiting teachers, from Zen masters to Jewish rabbis, as well as a few of their students, including British Vipassanā teacher Christopher Titmuss, American teacher Gabriel Cousens and two Tibetan Rinpoches. During that initial process, I built a list of ten questions, which I used as the basis of each interview and from which I happily diverted into whatever interesting subject came up during the talk. I soon discovered that teachers were generally clearer and had more to say than students about what it meant to be a student, based on their previous experience with their own teachers, so I devoted a good part of many of the interviews to the teachers' experiences as students.

After completing that first round of interviews in Israel, and with the generous help of *Buddha at the Gas Pump* interviewer Rick Archer, interfaith dialogue advocate Kurt Johnson and some of my friends in Europe and the United States, I began contacting teachers from other parts of the world and asking them for interviews about their relationships with their own teachers as well as with their students.

I was surprised by the high ratio of positive responses I received. Within a few months I had conducted about thirty more interviews, most of them via Skype and a few in face-to-face meetings during trips I made to the U.K. and the U.S. About half of the interviews were with teachers; the other half were follow-up conversations with their students. Reading through the interviews and considering the excerpts, I found that the most potent parts of each interview were those during which I sensed a paradox or an unresolved question or dilemma—all of which were suggested by an interviewee's hesitation, inconsistency, vagueness or confusion. One night over dinner, I excitedly told my wife that I came upon what would be the heart of my book: the paradoxes and dilemmas in the spiritual teacher-student relationship.

I became most interested in the types of relationships in which paradoxes and dilemmas were most prominent, including spiritual mentorships and root guru-disciple relationships, which are described in the next chapter. These relationships are characterized by a high level of commitment, involvement on many levels and a certain intensity of intimacy or love between teacher and student.

After conducting nearly one-hundred interviews, of which about one-third were with teachers and two-thirds were with students, and forming a list of about a dozen types of paradoxes and dilemmas, I decided to dedicate each chapter in this book to a specific problem and demonstrate it through one or two interviews in which it is most clearly evident. This meant that most of the interviews I conducted were not included in this book, but excerpts from many of them—as well as additional paradoxes and dilemmas that were not included—are posted on my website *The Freedom to Question* (free2quest.com).

THE FUNCTIONS AND CLASSIFICATIONS OF THE TEACHER-STUDENT RELATIONSHIP

There are four classifications of spiritual masters:
  the ordinary spiritual master,
  the bodhisattva spiritual master who has attained certain bhumis,
  the Nirmanakaya spiritual master, and
  the Sambhogakaya spiritual master.
These four types are related to an individual's spiritual realizations. When one is ordinary or just beginning, one cannot attend Buddhas and bodhisattvas who have attained higher levels as spiritual masters, so one attends an ordinary spiritual master. When one's karmic obscurations are more purified, one can attend a bodhisattva spiritual master who has attained higher levels. After one accomplishes the great accumulation path, one can attend a Nirmanakaya spiritual master. When one attains the bodhisattva's level, one can attend a Sambhogakaya spiritual master.

—GAMPOPA, *THE JEWEL ORNAMENT OF LIBERATION*

The first step... is to acknowledge certain empirical facts about student-teacher relationships. (1) Almost all spiritual seekers progress through stages along the spiritual path. (2) Most practitioners study with several teachers during their lifetimes and build up different relationships with each. (3) Not every spiritual teacher has reached the same level of accomplishment. (4) The type of relationship appropriate between a specific seeker and a specific teacher depends upon the spiritual level of each. (5) People usually relate to their teachers in progressively deeper manners as they advance along the spiritual path. (6) Because the same teacher may play different roles in the spiritual life of each seeker, the most appropriate relationship each seeker has with that teacher may [change].

—ALEXANDER BERZIN, *WISE TEACHER, WISE STUDENT*

Before we dive into the various paradoxes and dilemmas which are the heart of this book, it is useful to become acquainted with Alexander Berzin's classifications in *Wise Teacher, Wise Student*. The rationale for these classifications is provided by Gampopa Sonam Rinchen in *The Jewel Ornament of Liberation* as well as by Berzin. While Gampopa's and Berzin's classifications are specific to teacher-student relationships in the Buddhist path, they are readily applicable to other paths and traditions.

INFORMATION CONVEYANCE

This is the common type of relationship between teachers and students in schools and academic institutions, as well as in religious and spiritual contexts. Berzin describes this kind of relationship as follows: "Let us call someone who conveys information about Buddha's teachings from a withdrawn perspective a 'Buddhism professor.' A person who not merely sits in the audience, but who actually studies with such a Buddhism professor would be a 'student of Buddhism.'"

KNOWLEDGE APPLICATION

If the "information conveyance relationship" is comparable to the academic teacher-student relationship, this type is comparable to the master craftsman-apprentice relationship. Berzin refers to the "Dharma instructor," who is someone "who imparts the teachings from the point of view of their practical application to life, based on personal experience," and he describes the difference between the "Buddhism professor" and the "Dharma instructor" as follows:

> *"Buddhism professors teach information gained from texts or from Western scholarly research. In addition, they may have tried to figure out the meaning of the teachings intellectually and thus may also teach from intellectual insight and understanding. Dharma instructors also have some level of scriptural knowledge and teach accordingly. In addition, however, they explain from experiential insight and understanding, gained from putting the teachings into practice and from trying to apply them to life. Buddhism professors may also have experiential insight, but they do not usually convey these insights to others."*

SPIRITUAL MENTORSHIP

Berzin further describes a spiritual mentor as "someone who leads others along the graded path to enlightenment," and he distinguishes this relationship from the former two as follows:

> *"The Buddhist teachings differentiate between insights and realizations. An insight does not make a significant change in one's life, but may lead in that direction. A realization, on the other hand, whether it be partial or complete, actually produces a noticeable improvement that lasts. The distinction we are drawing here between Dharma instructors and spiritual mentors derives from this difference. Dharma instructors may have either insight or realization, whereas spiritual mentors need to have some level of realization...*
>
> *"Buddhism professors and Dharma instructors teach primarily through verbal instruction. For spiritual teachers to guide seekers fully, however, they need also to embody the teachings integrated into their personalities. Only then, as spiritual mentors, can they truly inspire and teach disciples by their living examples. Because of the obvious personal development of mentors, spiritual seekers feel confident in entrusting themselves as disciples to them, to help reach*

similar levels of self-transformation. Spiritual mentors, then, help disciples to develop their personalities."

ROOT GURU-DISCIPLE RELATIONSHIP

According to Berzin, "Root gurus are the spiritual mentors who turn disciples' hearts and minds most ardently to the Buddhist path. They are the strongest sources of inspiration to sustain disciples throughout their spiritual journeys. The relationships with such teachers act as roots for all attainments."

CHAPTER 1
THE NON-TEACHER TEACHER

I don't see myself as a teacher, although it certainly seems that I am. But for this interview, I am happy to pretend that I am teacher and speak as if I were.

—JAMES SWARTZ (FROM AN INTERVIEW)

I was once with a great Tibetan teacher, and a student asked him, "If all enlightenment is within you, why do you need a guru?" And he said, "You need a guru to tell you that you don't need a guru!"

—MIRABAI BUSH, FROM "OF TEACHERS AND TEACHING: WHO IS A TEACHER? WHAT IS A TEACHER?" *INSIGHT NEWSLETTER*, BARRE CENTER FOR BUDDHIST STUDIES, FALL 1993

PETER (HAKIM) YOUNG

My interview with Peter (Hakim) Young was the first one that I conducted. I had previously heard of Peter, the mild and gentle British successor of the colorful Turkish mystic Bulent Rauf, from several people who had stayed at the Beshara Centre. People spoke of there being a rarified atmosphere at the Chisholme Institute (the charity organization based at Beshara), but when I tried to get information about what was happening there, I couldn't get a clear picture—except that the food there was exceptionally good, and that it was Bulent, who passed away thirty years ago, who was responsible for that. So when I heard, through some friends, that Hakim was visiting Israel with his Israeli-born wife, I asked to meet with him, and he agreed.

AMIR: Would you tell me about your relationship with Bulent Rauf, your teacher?

HAKIM: I'll start by saying that Bulent never regarded himself as a teacher. He used to say, "There is only one teacher [pointing upwards], and I'm a fellow student, just like you."

AMIR: How do you understand that?

HAKIM: I think there are two levels of his "not being a teacher." The first one is that reality itself, or what we might call "God," is the only teacher. All guidance ultimately comes from that single source. To give a simple example, I might be a plumber and I'm in a situation where I don't know how to fix something; then I discover how to do it. I would consider the guidance even for that discovery as coming from that one source.

AMIR: Would you also say that knowing itself, before knowing anything specific, comes from that source?

HAKIM: Absolutely. All knowledge is single-sourced, therefore all guidance is single-sourced and it's diffused into everything according to the capacity of that thing. For example, you and I have different individual capacities. The guidance that comes to me will be according to my relative capacity to receive and in line with my unique destiny. My relative capacity can also be expanded, when I tune in to what's there for me. That's the place of the teacher in this world, to help me to reach my uniqueness.

AMIR: What is the other level of "not being a teacher"?

HAKIM: I think that Bulent is more than a teacher. Some people who we know as "teachers" help others to come to the single source, yet they are not themselves embodying that source. Bulent was actually embodying the source, which is why he said that it was not him that was the teacher. So on the one hand, there is the metaphysical Truth that there is only one teacher, and, on the other hand, there are those who embody the reality of that metaphysical Truth. I think he is one of those.

AMIR: Could it also be that him saying, "There is only one teacher and I'm a fellow student," was his way of turning the student's attention from him personally to the source?

HAKIM: I think so, yes. But it wasn't a trick. His taste was not to be a teacher, but rather to be genuinely, truly nothing. He wanted to be under the constantly changing revelation of the reality. If you are already a knower, you can't be that; but if you're a student of reality, then you're learning moment by moment. So his saying that he was a student was not diminishing himself, but elevating the meaning of being a student, to being a receiver and open to the divine guidance.

AMIR: So the teacher, in the case of Bulent, was actually teaching by being an example of "studentship" of the source, of that higher knowledge.

HAKIM: That's right. He wasn't teaching. He was simply being.

AMIR: Could you tell me what led to your meeting with Bulent? Were you looking for a teacher?

HAKIM: This was in the early '70s. I was twenty-four years old, living in the material world, working more than full time, basically living somebody else's life. Then I had this car accident and a kind of near-death experience during it. I was recovering when a friend arrived at my doorstep and said to me, "I really think you should go to this place." This was the first time that I had heard of the Beshara Centre, which was at a place called Swyre Farm in Gloucestershire. I went there for a weekend, and that visit awakened something in me. I went back home, thought about that for a while and then got together with some people who'd also been in that place, and we met for study and meditation, etc. In one of my subsequent visits to Swyre Farm, I first met Bulent.

AMIR: Was it a love at first sight?

HAKIM: No, my involvement and relationship with him developed gradually, over years. Eventually, I moved to Chisholme House, in Scotland, which was being renovated and turned into the Beshara School. Bulent was there for a lot of the time. He didn't teach but he was a consultant, guiding the people who were running the courses. I joined the first course there and for me it was an absolutely life-changing experience. I remember saying to myself, "I want to be involved in this; this is the path for me." Then Bulent asked me to be involved with the next course as a facilitator, and after that I participated in a follow-up six-month course. For that course, Bulent was fully present nearly all of the time. He warned us at the outset: "For this course, you'll be under the whims of a grumpy old man." I must say I found it really difficult. It was so intense. We were meeting for conversation with Bulent every day without exception for maybe six hours a day. Extraordinary things came out during those six months. We were introduced to a place that we can't own, but if we're fortunate we can gain access to it—a place of journeying.

I'll make a long leap here to 1984, when I was invited to come and be the director of studies for the six-month course, and afterwards I was appointed principal of the school. That summer Bulent was unwell when he came back from Turkey, and when he was diagnosed with cancer he told me, "I want you to look after me."

AMIR: Was it only then that the relationship between you became closer?

HAKIM: Yes. I think that an invitation from him to come closer had been there much earlier, but I had been too afraid and held myself back. But at that point, in 1984, there was no choice. Or rather, there had been a choice but I'd already made it, so that then there was no choice. He said, "Come closer." I said yes. Then I was in agreement. It wasn't always easy, in fact it was very intense at times, but I had agreed to sit down in the fire.

AMIR: What was the intensity? Do you think he deliberately put pressure on you, or was it more of a spontaneous result of being in his presence?

HAKIM: There is a poem by Rumi about a conversation between a chickpea and the cook cooking it, which is a metaphor for the teacher-student relationship. Well, Bulent was preparing me for the role and for the responsibilities I had agreed to take. It was a highly pressurized situation. I was cooked, mashed and reshaped by him into nice hummus!

It's important to clarify at this point that none of this would have been possible without my permission. And my permission was an essential one, from my essence. You could say it was my essential request, which is that I wanted to get closer to the *real*, I wanted to be of service, I wanted to be completely under divine love. Well, if that's the case, then certain things have to happen and some of them are going to be a little painful. This is not a caravan of pain, but pain is part of the growing. That's what the cook says to the chickpea: "If you want to be nice, soft and delicious, if you want to realize your essential goodness, then stay in the pot." Of course, if that essential request had not been present it might have looked like a sort of bullying. But it was not.

AMIR: Were there times in which you felt that the pressure was too much for you?

HAKIM: There were times when I felt completely crushed, but it's interesting that, although being with him was sometimes like sitting in the middle of a volcano, for some reason you never felt that he was out to destroy you. Something always felt right, even though your limbs and appendages were getting chopped off. We also had a lot of fun. He had a great sense of humor and we laughed a lot. Sometimes we'd be helplessly rolling over with laughter, crying with laughter, unable to breathe...

AMIR: What was it like for you when he died?

HAKIM: It was a very mixed period. There was the real sorrow that something has come to an end, but there was also this feeling of extraordinary joy, which was bodily joy, it didn't come from a thought. A real grounded experience of joy which I'd never experienced before.

AMIR: How do you understand that?

HAKIM: When Rumi departed, he said to his followers, "Don't grieve for me, this is only my nutshell. I'm going to rejoin my beloved." You see, while we're here, however much we talk about the union with the beloved, we're still under the conditions of relativity and a kind of a distance, a trace of separation remains. When you die, or return to the source, there is the joy of reunion. Because it's real and it's not just his, not just Bulent's, the whole universe experiences it. Something has become completed in the most beautiful way. It was tremendous.

AMIR: Do you feel that he has continued to guide you in some way, to function as your teacher, even after his passing away?

HAKIM: Yes, but when you say "he," we have to go back to the single source which he represented. I believe it was him, but what is *him*? That question needs to be asked just as I need to ask, "Who am I?" If I'm asking, "Who am I?" I need to ask, "Who is he?" as well. Of course, that guidance is not limited to him. It can come from anywhere and it can still be him, but in another form. Do you see what I'm saying?

AMIR: I do, but don't you find there's something in your relationship with Bulent that makes this guidance more accessible to you?

HAKIM: That's right, and I'll tell you how that continues today. A *maqam*, a physical place or spiritual point of reference, is important for us all to find. For me, it is the Monument to Man at Chisholme, where Bulent is buried. I am fortunate that I can go there anytime, even if only in my intention. It has become a place of imagination within my intention. The fact that it's in my imagination doesn't mean that it's not real. Real things happen there, in this place of the imagination, just like being with somebody in the flesh. So, yes, guidance continues. It doesn't have to be at the monument, but the monument is for me a very useful physical representation of this guidance. When I visit, I am reminded of who I am and I am returned to who I am. All the peripheral stuff, the petty concerns, even if they don't drop away immediately, they become reduced, and a different perspective is given. So, yes, guidance continues.

In preparation for my meeting with Hakim, I searched online for information about Bulent, and what I found fascinated me. The description of him on the Chisholme Institute website begins like this: "Bulent Rauf (1911–87) was a man who escaped definition deliberately, but whom many varied descriptions fitted easily: a gentleman, a mystic, a world-class cook, archaeologist, writer and translator, Turkish citizen and man of the world, lover of beauty and champion of esoteric education."

I learned that British mystic and author Reshad Field considered Bulent to be his teacher, and that Field's well-known book *The Last Barrier—A True Story of a Journey into Ultimate Reality* was about their relationship. I also stumbled upon a documentary, *In Search of Oil and Sand*, released in 2012, which tells a fable-like story about how Bulent, who was married to Princess Faiza, the sister of King Farouk of Egypt, created in 1952 with members of the Egyptian royal family and their friends an amateur movie, *Oil and Sand*, whose plot predicted with uncanny precision the coup d'état in which King Farouk was ousted—which happened only a few months later. I came to the meeting with Hakim eager to hear about his relationship with that remarkable man, and I wasn't disappointed.

I chose to start the book with this interview not only because it was the first one I conducted, but also because it touches on one of the most basic questions that has always baffled me: *Why would a teacher tell their students that he or she is not a teacher, that they don't need and must not have a teacher or that there is absolutely nothing to teach or learn? Why would anybody make such patently self-contradictory claims?*

This paradox was especially evident for me in regard to the powerfully awake and profoundly influential J. Krishnamurti. Videos of him speaking to an audience or conversing with someone, not only with great conviction and confidence but also with powerful authority, leave little question in my mind that, if anybody should be regarded as a spiritual teacher, it is he. So why did he often use his spiritual weight and charisma to assert that there is no teacher and no pupil, and got upset when people referred to him as a teacher or even implied that?

These questions were highlighted also in the way Hakim spoke about his relationship with Bulent. It seems clear to me that Bulent functioned as and was a teacher to him and to his peers. Even the reasons that Hakim gave, for that not being the case, actually explained why Bulent *was* indeed a teacher and expressed Hakim's great appreciation for that.

In Mariana Caplan's *The Guru Question: The Perils and Rewards of Choosing a Spiritual Teacher*, she dedicated a section in her chapter entitled "Types of Spiritual Authority" to this paradox; there, she writes:

> *An increasing number of teachers say they are not teachers. There are many reasons for taking this position. In many of the contemporary neo-Advaita-Vedanta nondual traditions, for example, the labels of "teacher" and "student" are often considered illusory distinctions within the nondual truth of oneness, and therefore obstacles to the nondual realization of oneness. This model suggests that the affirmation of the teacher outside of oneself often distracts the practitioner from the truth of the inner teacher or guru, and disempowers the student's self-awakening and the cultivation of trust in her own inner authority.*
>
> *The point of discernment to be aware of in this circumstance is as follows: When two people are functioning as teacher and student*

*in the Western world, there is an almost inevitable arising of psy-
chological projections and power dynamics in spite of what a teacher does or does not call him or herself; and when the student-teacher
relationship is not acknowledged or well structured, built-in structures to help both the student and teacher navigate the psychological complexities that arise for each of them often go lacking.*

I will end the presentation of this paradox with the answer that
Andrew Cohen (in Chapter 12) gave me in one of the interviews I
did with him for this book, when I asked him why he thought
Krishnamurti insisted he was not a teacher.

ANDREW COHEN

ANDREW: I think that's because Krishnamurti was aware of the
transference and projection that too often happens when people
meet genuinely enlightened teachers. He wanted people to take responsibility for themselves and be mature. He was reacting to many
of the difficult problems that tend to arise around powerful and
charismatic spiritual teachers. Ironically, while he was doing this,
he was denying who he really was. He himself was brilliant, radiant and obviously deeply enlightened. He liked to pretend he was
not any different than anybody else, but it wasn't true, and he knew
it. He knew he was in touch with a level of depth and heightened
consciousness that most people are oblivious to. And to be honest,
when someone is so much more awake than others, they can't really
hide it. It's not only obvious to them, but to all others who have the
eyes to see. The light of consciousness shines through them with so
much more power, depth and intelligence that it's almost unavoidable. The "Guru Principle" was alive and active in that extraordinary
man, even though he did his very best to appear to be no different
than anyone else.

CHAPTER 2
SPIRITUAL FRIEND OR GURU?

The disciple must resort to the feet of a wise teacher, one who is an embodiment of that Teacher Who is already in his heart, the Eternal Wisdom.... [H]e needs the guidance of one who, because his whole being has become one with the Wisdom, can speak with the same voice as that Teacher in the heart and yet can do so in tones which can be heard with the outer ear.

—SRI KRISHNA PREM, *THE YOGA OF THE BHAGAVAT GITA*

[The Buddha] stated that the Dharma teacher acts as a spiritual friend (kalyana mitta) as well as an authority figure since the teacher belongs to the Sangha of practitioners.

—CHRISTOPHER TITMUSS, *THE BUDDHA OF LOVE*

First and foremost, a teacher is not a friend. If we really want to awaken, we do not need friendship but rather more unpredictability.

—THOMAS HÜBL, INTEGRALESFORUM.ORG

STEPHEN FULDER

Stephen Fulder was one of my early interviewees. We met for the interview at the Tovana Sangha House in Tel Aviv, where he spends a couple of days a week, a three-hour bus ride from his home in the Upper Galilee. *Tovana*, the Hebrew word for Vipassanā or "insight," is the name of a leading Buddhist practice organization in Israel, which Stephen founded more than thirty years ago, and where he functions as a senior Dharma teacher. The apartment's cool air and quiet and serene atmosphere were a relief from the hot, busy city streets outside, whose sounds were muffled by the closed windows and the hiss of the air conditioner.

AMIR: Let's start with you as a student—who were your teachers or people you still consider as your teachers nowadays?

STEPHEN: In the Theravada tradition that I've been practicing and involved with, the principle of a single primary teacher—root guru or *Satguru*—is not relevant, and so I've had plenty of teachers. My first teacher was S.N. Goenka, but the relationship with him was impersonal, as he was teaching thousands of students. In Goenka's tradition, based on a Burmese lineage, the teachers teach the practice rather technically and don't really relate to you as an individual and to your issues or your life. They are masters at passing on to you a technique and motivating and encouraging you to practice intensively.

AMIR: But even though you say there was no personal relationship with Goenka and he was just communicating the teaching in a very technical way, there was something about him that made him a better vehicle for the teaching than many other teachers in that tradition. There was a reason why you went to see him and not hundreds of other teachers. What I'm aiming at is that there is something about the person that is an important factor in the transmission of the teaching.

STEPHEN: Yes, I only did one retreat with Goenka himself, who is charismatic and inspiring, and after that I did about a dozen with Sayama. She came from the same tradition as Goenka, and they both had the same teacher. Why I kept going back to her is an interesting question. I think it's because she embodied a very finely tuned and subtle understanding of practice. I really respected her extraordinary power of mind, her Samadhi, and how she brought this into the practice. There was something about her that was crystal clear—as if she was coming from a subtle awareness and a space that I could trust, that did not embody a lot of belief or tradition or control. She radiated a present moment awareness that was very big, free, unbounded, powerful and deserved respect.

Also, Sayama was one of the few teachers I met in my life that clearly had extraordinary powers. She would often answer my questions before I asked them. I would come into her room with a question in my mind and she would immediately start to answer it and so I didn't need to say anything. So in terms of a student-teacher relationship there was definitely more content, flow and dynamism than the relationship with Goenka.

AMIR: Would you say that in your relationship with Sayama there was a spiritual intimacy or deep connection? Because what you described about her ability to know what's on your mind and respond—that must have something to do with knowing each other very well or communicating on a deep level.

STEPHEN: Not exactly. There was deep communication but it was not at all personal. It was technique oriented. She didn't know me or was interested in me as Stephen, with a certain character and personality. I don't think she really cared about me that much. She was dedicated to understanding and guiding my experiences, on a specific well-trodden path within the frame of reference of the practice. There is a benefit in this dedication, but also a cost, since it is a bit like a parent only relating to their child according to how well they do at school. A lot will be missing, for example the ability to know the gifts and inner life of each person and so guide the practice more holistically and individually.

Since then, I've met many teachers who I sat with and talked to, and though I wouldn't say they were major teachers in my life, they certainly helped me on the road. Some of those really did have a much more personal relationship with me, such that in a way we never forgot each other. There are a few who I would say have been more significant guides, friends and co-travelers along the way, including Fred von Allman, Joseph Goldstein and particularly Christopher Titmuss, who I have been close to for more than thirty years, and for whom I have enormous respect and appreciation as a friend, a teacher and a colleague.

I want to stress that teaching happens at several levels at once, not all of which may be consciously known by the student. There is the guiding in which the teacher as a kind of tour guide defines the path and the way and supports the student along it. There is the imparting of verbal knowledge, inspiration and hints of what is beyond. There is the modeling, in which the teacher radiates a more invisible way of being. Teaching can also happen when the teacher mirrors or reflects back to you something you asked or did, offering a larger, freer and wiser perspective, and in that moment they become teachers of yours, although it's not consciously a teacher-student relationship in any way. Once I was in India on a six-week self-retreat, in a small room in an ashram, and there was a spiritual teacher teaching in a nearby ashram. He used to come to my room at 5:30 in the morning every couple of days and we would sit and talk. He would first of all kiss my feet, which is of course an Indian way of expressing his appreciation for my practice, and I bowed to his feet as well because the appreciation was mutual. Then we would talk and I felt that any question I threw out was answered from a huge space, as if throwing a pebble into a great clay jar and listening to the unlimited resonances. You could feel that space behind his eyes, from which I was seen and understood. The words could be about rice and beans or about the subtlest and most delicate movements in consciousness. Everything that was put in there came back out spontaneously, immediately, with no obvious thought behind it, emerging like an echo from this expanded awareness.

He's not my teacher and I did not see him before or after that, but we had something very powerful, intimate and unforgettable that went on between us. I was clearly in the role of student and he was in the role of teacher. Maybe in another time it could have been reversed, where I might've helped him, but that was the framework we chose and kind of agreed on without words, and we were both happy with that.

AMIR: You're really giving a few very different examples or models of the teacher-student relationship.

STEPHEN: Yes, teaching can be much more existential than sitting on a stage and giving talks. It can be with the eyes, with body language, with the way you are with people, with how you sing to a baby or how you relate to a dog or a cat in the street—and that's teaching. On a subtle level, it is teaching because it's coming from that expanded awareness and clarity and wisdom that I was talking about, manifesting naturally within ordinary life. I feel that people who are quite developed teach that way. They don't always teach as intentionally and consistently, it might be quite spontaneous and actually they can't do anything else. This doesn't need a label—but it is teaching.

AMIR: I think you're saying that for some people the formality of a defined teacher-student interrelation can enhance their ability, pull out of them greater depth, responsibility, care, etc., while for others, it may do the opposite and actually be an obstacle.

STEPHEN: That's right. In many cases, it is really needed to start off, as it sets the scene, defines the territory of teaching and is familiar to students, a bit like going back to school. Thus it is an agreement that reduces the concerns and insecurities of the unknown. But indeed, there are some students who don't really need this theatre and for whom the projections and roles of teacher and student are just a nuisance. More than that, it may trigger psychological resistance and friction, perhaps because of some previous pain connected with their relationship with "father." In any case, the formality and the separation and the roles gradually break down along the way, and then the word "teacher" becomes irrelevant. When you talk about a deeper level, the roles, concepts and words tend to break down and cease to function as a medium of teaching. One should be aware of that. The teaching then happens naturally because nothing else can happen, and it is expressed in speech, body and mind. There isn't anything that a teacher needs to do, he or she is manifesting their spirituality through themselves. The role vanishes, and there is no thought that says: "I'm going to teach now. Look at the way I'm walking down the corridor."

AMIR: And yet you seem okay with being called a teacher, you seem comfortable being in that position and fulfilling that function—why is that? Are there any benefits, psychological or spiritual, that you get from being a teacher?

STEPHEN: For sure. The importance is in the doing of it, not in the label, which is not interesting. If I am called a teacher or not called a teacher, it doesn't turn a hair. One benefit for me is that the expression or teaching of the dharma releases more of the stream. Teaching moves through me and out, so I feel the flow and that's joyful, and that's one reason why I keep teaching. Another reason is that there is nothing more interesting for me to do in life.

What else is there? Go to the office every day and do an ordinary job? It's so joyful to be in the environment of the teaching situation and to be creative and playful. It brings out of me qualities that are needed in this struggling world, so I think it's what I can do to help the world. Another benefit I feel is that teaching simply opens the heart in the present moment meetings with an individual or even a group. In the last year I have been going 'round pubs and bars, under the title "Buddha at the Bar," giving talks and meditations to large numbers of people, and it warms the heart to bring a different message to young people who are often so much in need of a more hopeful and meaningful view beyond the usual diet of conflict, materialism, competitiveness, pressure and agitation.

AMIR: I think you're saying that to have the right relationship to what comes out of you as a teacher means that you have to let go of any sense of possessing the teaching.

STEPHEN: Yes, definitely. You let go of possessing the teaching, of owning the role, and in the same way you let go of you possessing yourself—the self that's on stage. You have to let go of that. The Dalai Lama expresses this very beautifully before giving teachings by symbolically bowing down to the seat before sitting on it. It's a ritual that says, "I'm going to sit on that seat and honor the role given to me, but I wear the role like clothes, and then come down and take the clothes off." Someone once told me that being a Dharma teacher is not about giving the most charismatic and wonderful talk you can give; but if you give the worst talk ever, you get up from your seat and have no more thoughts about it.

AMIR: Do you think that, as the Dalai Lama sits on his seat and wears those clothes, he also activates in himself certain human qualities that are required of anyone in that role? Is that something you experience when you sit on the stage in front of people asking you questions, that certain human qualities manifest in you that don't manifest in other situations?

STEPHEN: No, I don't think there are qualities I don't have in other situations too, but certainly conditions will pull out of you and emphasize particular qualities that are needed and fitting to that situation. For example, the condition of running—I run every couple of days—pulls out of me qualities of perseverance. Teaching enhances sensitivity in a few dimensions. It invites me to be particularly caring and very watchful, and not to talk unkindly or unwisely; [to be] more watchful or mindful than perhaps I am with my grandchildren. Then, it encourages me to develop qualities of steadiness and confidence as well as fine-tuned ethics and care, clarity of mind, kindness, confidence and a little bit of authority. I'm given the authority and I am aware of that and appreciate it so I hold it with tenderness and some respect. Maybe there's also a lift in energy that comes from being on the stage—a lift of the heart, I would say.

AMIR: Would you say that you are spiritually elevated as you step into that position?

STEPHEN: In a way, yes, but there are many other situations in life when I also feel that. So it's definitely not the only one. I might feel that also in the deep silence of early morning before sunrise, when everything is quiet and I can only hear the jackals far away. So it's not only in the teacher role, but the conditions of the teaching do tend to elevate you to the best you can be. Yes, I do feel that.

AMIR: How do you feel or respond when people say to you that you are their teacher, or they ask you to be their teacher?

STEPHEN: I don't prevent it. I don't tell people they must not say that about me—I can't. But I don't at all encourage it. I don't support exclusivity in today's modern culture, and I suggest to students to learn from many teachers. Sometimes when people say to me, "I want you to be my teacher," I say to them, "Okay, I don't mind you regarding me as being the main teacher for the moment, but I don't really like the label, and eventually you should have other teachers as well." I tend to discourage exclusivity whether in relation to myself or other teachers because I think it reduces the autonomy, the independence of mind and the authenticity and confidence of the student.

The other thing is that I don't want to be constantly available for those who expect me to be in that role all the time. The role of personal teacher would carry with it an obligation. I just don't want to be disturbed when I'm not teaching, like when I'm in my vegetable garden. I actually don't want people calling me with questions like, "Should I go to India?" or "Should I get married?" or "Should I change jobs?" I am fine if they ask me those questions in the context of retreats and teaching, and then I'd relate to them, but that's it, and then I go home and I take off that role like peeling off well-worn clothes.

AMIR: This is solving quite a few problems that other models of teacher-student relationship have, but also, don't you think—and you've met a lot of people along the path—that for some people, the position of surrender, of trusting somebody else very deeply, more than they trust themselves, is an important catalyst in their journey?

STEPHEN: It can indeed be helpful, but only if it's light. If it's too intense and total, it can undo their spiritual journey, because they're replacing themselves with someone else. But of all the questions you have asked so far, this is the most problematic and nuanced. Because, on the one hand, you can say, "What's wrong with praying to the Buddha as a larger-than-life figure, identifying with and respecting his qualities, and so letting the prayer to the Buddha remind you of your own Buddha qualities?" But it only works if it is quite light. If there is a strong sense of supplication, worship, glorification and deification of a teacher or an icon, it can disempower our practice and disconnect us from our spiritual sources. Where I feel it's too much, I would tend to question it and bring it back down to size. I would tend to say to the person, "You're going too far making the teacher unrealistically dominant, using projection onto the teacher to avoid meeting your own existential pain and joy, and I suggest you go back to yourself a little bit." I think it's the scale—when trust and dependence on a teacher goes over the top it almost begins to be pathological.

In our Theravada tradition, we would tend to constantly shift the focus from the teacher to the teaching, the Dharma itself. I would tend to say: "Take refuge in the Dharma, not in Stephen." This is different from the guru tradition, where the guru would be happy to hold that place of dependence for longer, to allow more intensity of transference. But it's a good question, and not black and white.

Of all that we spoke about, it was Stephen's story about his relationship with the man he met on his self-retreat in India, whom he described as being "half my peer and to some extent a teacher," that stirred me most and stayed with me longest after the interview was over. His description of a fluid, informal, free and dynamic teacher-student relationship had the flavor of a fairytale—a fairytale I knew at the beginning of my relationship with Andrew and I still long for. Can a relationship such as the one he described, be maintained, or is it only the stuff that summer flings are made of?

I became most interested in the possibility of flexibility and variability in the teacher-student relationship, and I explored the guru/spiritual friend dynamic with many of the interviewees: Does the teacher hold different hierarchical positions in their relationship with different students? Are they comfortable playing either the "guru" and the "friend" roles, or do they have a strong preference to one or the other? Do they readily adjust and change position in their relationship with any specific student?

For some of the interviewees, there seemed to be little dynamic to speak of. This was clearly the case with Andrew Cohen (Chapter 7). During the time I was his student, the relationship between him and his students at that time could be characterized as "absolute hierarchy." On the opposite end of the spectrum, the egalitarian model of the "spiritual friend" was expounded upon by Vipassanā teacher Christopher Titmuss in my interview with him.

CHRISTOPHER TITMUSS

CHRISTOPHER: Many teachers stick to their role—they teach a retreat or give a public talk and keep to their private life. I prefer to develop good friendships in the Sangha. I appreciate the Buddha's encouragement to develop *kalyana mitta,* which essentially means "good friend." Just before you arrived to interview me, I went out with two good Dharma friends to eat together. I regard such informal contact as vitally important in terms of the social aspect of the Sangha. I enjoy informal friendship. I think it's very helpful for the students—although I don't use the word "students" very often. I prefer to use the words "yogis" or "practitioners" or the "Sangha." It is equally important for them and for me to experience informal contact. I get the chance to know them as a friend, but equally, they get to know me. I don't think we need to elevate ourselves as an archetype, namely the spiritual teacher sitting in a role. Such a formal, functional approach is fine and it has its place, but it is also valuable to know a teacher in an informal way through a whole variety of situations. This develops a real connection. This is what I do and who I am.

JAMES FINLEY

Finally, an exchange related to the interplay between the functions of a spiritual friend and a guru took place during my interview with James Finley. As a young monk at the monastery of the Abbey of Gethsemane, James received spiritual guidance from the renowned monk and author Thomas Merton, and nowadays James leads spiritual retreats and works as a private clinical psychologist. In my interview with him, which took place over Skype, we both experienced a tangible sense of intimacy and friendship with each other, and out of that came the following exchange:

JAMES: Let's take, for example, us talking right now. We're sitting here together, two human beings participating in mutual exploration, attempting to shed light on the unexplainable nature of the unitive mystery. So that's happening right now with us. Now let's assume that toward the end of our time together you say: "Jim, before we go I have a personal question that I'd like to consult you about." Let's say you'd ask and I would listen out of the way we've been just talking and respond, but I'd say, "Well if you don't mind I also have a question for you: this is something that I am going through in my life, my wife and I are talking about death and the fear of losing each other," and you'd listen to me. And then we'd both say to each other: thank you! So you see, this space between us holds endless variations, like the wind goes as it pleases.

AMIR: That's beautiful! Now let's compare it with a different scenario, in which I set up a meeting with you because I want to consult you as my teacher. I think our stance toward each other would be slightly different, and that would make something possible between us, that is different from us having a friendly conversation.

JAMES: Let's say, you call because you want to speak to me in my role as a teacher, then I have to meet you by serving that role. If you're in the role of the student, I have to be willing to be in the role of the teacher. Then the whole exploration would be in that context, of a teacher-student exchange. What is it in the exchange that you're counting for me as the teacher to teach? I have to be faithful to the lineage and heritage of the tradition. I have to be sitting there and letting it use me for its own purposes. I have to be there for you with the integrity of that.

CHAPTER 3
PERSONAL AND IMPERSONAL

Well, there's also an element in some teachers, almost an effort to disappear, to truly embody the teachings. And these were the teachers with whom it was most confusing, because you knew there was a person in there somewhere.

—**SHARON SALZBERG**, FROM "OF TEACHERS AND TEACHING: WHO IS A TEACHER? WHAT IS A TEACHER?" *INSIGHT NEWSLETTER*

The guru function is, in essence, impersonal. It is not about the personality of the student or the teacher. This is a particularly difficult reality for the student to wrap his or her mind around when the felt experience of the relationship between student and teacher is the most deeply personal bond of love and reverence he or she has ever known. Yet the impersonal nature of this bond is precisely why it produces a quality of feeling and a possibility of exchange rarely found elsewhere in the human experience. It is nothing other than God loving God, Truth loving Truth. In the words of Daniel Moran, "Absolute intimacy is absolutely impersonal."

—**MARIANA CAPLAN**, *THE GURU QUESTION*

When you discover the real relationship with your teacher you discover that there is no other. It's paradoxical, but you actually need the other to realize that there is no other.

—LAURA WILLIAMS (FROM AN INTERVIEW WITH WILLIAMS, A STUDENT OF CYNTHIA BAMPTON)

LLEWELLYN VAUGHAN-LEE

The paradox of the personal/impersonal or relative/absolute nature of the teacher-student relationship has been front and center for me ever since I was catapulted into a state of unitive consciousness, in which there was no I, no other and no relationship; and at the same (no-)time, I also realized that Andrew Cohen had always been and would always be my Teacher. How can the absolute-impersonal and the relative-personal be so closely—inseparably—related?

I posed this question to many of the interviewees, and it turned out to be alive, present and paradoxical for most. It was clearly central in my interview with Sufi master Llewellyn Vaughan-Lee, a student of Irina Tweedie, and her lineage successor in the Naqshbandiyya Sufi Order.

AMIR: What does being a teacher mean to you?

LLEWELLYN: To be a teacher is to be in service to the path and the work of the path. I have been given the duty to be the representative of a Naqshbandi Sufi tradition, and as such I have been given access to the transmission of the path, the energy, the grace that is needed for the disciple to progress on the path. On this Sufi path, the transmission is a quality of divine love, or grace. My work, my responsibility, is to keep this transmission pure and help the wayfarer to be aligned to the path and give them the energy, the love, that is needed to realize their highest spiritual potential. We say that the ego cannot go beyond the ego, the mind cannot go beyond the mind, so on their own, the student does not have the energy or guidance to make the journey.

AMIR: What are some of the differences you see between you and your students?

LLEWELLYN: Spiritually, the student needs everything from the teacher, while the teacher is not allowed to want anything from the student. The teacher is one who has been made empty, has become featureless and formless. The student—particularly in the initial years—will often project their higher self or divine nature onto the teacher, which is a very powerful and numinous projection. The teacher has to bear the projections of the student, both positive and negative, while the teacher should not project anything onto the student.

AMIR: You say that the teacher is not allowed to want anything from the student, but doesn't the teacher need *something* from the student—not for himself, but so that he can fulfill his function? I'm thinking of honesty, respect, appreciation, trust, even love—doesn't the teacher need and want them?

LLEWELLYN: This is an interesting question, and also distinguishes between *need* and *want*. As I mentioned, this is a path of freedom, and so the wayfarer must be left free, and the teacher must want nothing on an essential level. And yet, in order for the teacher to do his or her work, a certain attitude on the part of the wayfarer is needed. What I have found is that a quality of respect is what is most important, and often most lacking in Western wayfarers—respect for the real nature of the teacher and the work that needs to be done. Without this respect there is little container for the inner work, and the *nafs* [the lower self] and personal psychological dynamics interfere too much. But it is not the teacher's personal self that is respected, but the role or position that the teacher has been given, as representative of a tradition.

You ask about love—and, yes, in our tradition, love is essential. The disciple progresses through love. Again, it is not a personal love, but a quality of divine love. If there is no love on their part, either he or she is not suited to this path, or the teacher has not been able to open or reach their heart as yet.

AMIR: You say that in your tradition, love is essential, but what does love actually mean if, as you said earlier, the teacher has become empty, featureless and formless? I guess you're using the word "love" in a very different way than it's usually thought of.

LLEWELLYN: This love is a quality of divine love—and, yes, it is very different to what most people identify as love. It is given directly from heart to heart, from soul to soul. But it is important to understand that this love is not personal. It is both intimate and impersonal.

This is a mystical tradition, the *via negativa*, that leads from the created to the uncreated, to the primal emptiness. One of the mysteries of the Sufi path is how the disciple is absorbed into the emptiness within the teacher. This process of absorption is an essential part of the final stages of the journey, which can also be described as merging within the teacher. On their own, the wayfarer cannot make the journey into the mystical emptiness. Through the empty heart of the teacher, the wayfarer is taken from existence to non-existence.

AMIR: Let me ask it this way: How important is the student's personal relationship with the teacher?

LLEWELLYN: Because this connection happens on the level of the soul, it has nothing to do with a personal relationship. In fact, I actively discourage people from trying to make a personal relationship with me, as it confuses the real nature of the love that is given and the soul connection. However, I have found that in the West, students, particularly female students, often want to have a personal relationship, to feel a personal connection.

There can be no personal friendship with the teacher, despite the feelings of inner closeness that are very real. The teacher is in essence an empty space, through which the energy of the divine can nourish the disciple, or a mirror that just reflects back our true self. Having no conscious understanding of its real nature, the disciple will color this soul relationship with personal dramas, with the images of parents or other authority figures, or even with the longing for a physical lover. She will paint her own pictures on this clear mirror.

Hopefully the teacher has been emptied so completely that there is no danger of being caught in the trap of so many projections. I was fortunate in that I was trained for almost twenty years before I began. I was ground to dust in order to do this work. And for the first few years I was watched very closely, and then crushed again. I was taught the old-fashioned way, forced to see my limitations again and again. And this was only the beginning.

AMIR: Can you say more about being ground to dust? Is this also part of the process that some of your students undergo?

LLEWELLYN: According to the ancient tradition, "one has to become less than the dust at the feet of the teacher," and this was also my experience with my teacher. One becomes nothing, worthless, without dignity or shame. One cares for nothing. It is completely brutal and ruthless and involves the whole person. For example, at the beginning I was not allowed to sleep for more than two or three hours every night, after which my kundalini energy awoke me. After months of this, you do not care about anything, you are ground down.

With most of my students, it is the power of love that transforms them, so I have only done this on very rare occasions, and only when it was absolutely necessary in order for the student to progress. Of course, there needs to be a degree of trust, as the disciple needs to be held in love while this takes place; otherwise, the psyche can be fractured. Even so, it still takes a long time, often years, for the psyche to heal from this process, unless the disciple is surrendered on all levels, which is very, very rare. But this is a terrible task for me as a teacher, because, on a human level, I care for my students and the suffering they may experience. I have not actually done this for many years now. Maybe I am getting too old or too soft! Though at times I do need to be strict, to point out mistakes or if they are going against the tradition.

AMIR: On the one hand, it sounds like the teacher has to be detached from their students, but you also spoke of love and care, and to me it sounds like ambivalence—is it?

LLEWELLYN: Here you touch part of the real paradox of being a teacher, of being completely involved and yet also detached. The spiritual heart of the wayfarer is held within the spiritual heart of the teacher, and so one cares on a very deep, soul level, both for the human suffering and happiness—illness, a fight with cancer, a baby born, child or grandchild—but [one cares] even more that the wayfarer can make this journey, that the soul can realize its highest potential. Because one knows of the real meaning of the soul's journey, one feels a deep fulfillment at the steps that are taken, and sadness at the missed opportunities. This is why the disciples are often described as the sheikh's spiritual family. Many of my disciples have been with me for fifteen, twenty years or more, and so I have come to care deeply about them also on a very human level.

And yet, without detachment and freedom, the journey could not take place, in the same way that real compassion requires detachment. This is a detachment that encompasses commitment and involvement, quite different, for example, from the detachment of a therapist. It is the inner detachment of real love, because the heart must belong only to God, otherwise the teacher could not help the student, would be as caught in the illusions of the world. In Sufism, the doorway to this is annihilation and "poverty of the heart"—having nothing and wanting nothing.

AMIR: Do you find that your students tend to delegate some of their responsibility to you? Do they lose some of their independence because they are in a relationship with you?

LLEWELLYN: Initially, the relationship—in which one may feel loved, accepted, recognized for the first time—can evoke dynamics of dependence. And it is only too easy to look to the teacher for guidance, to project onto the teacher one's own inner guidance.

But I have found that, in most instances, the energy and practices of the path push the wayfarer to stand on their own feet, to claim their own inner guidance. Often there is a period of feeling completely alone, even abandoned by the teacher and the path. This is a test that requires the wayfarer to journey inwardly beyond patterns of dependence and claim their own relationship to the self. If a serious student remains too attached, they find themselves ignored or even "thrown out of the group" for a length of time, maybe a year or two, so that they have to find their own feet, their own inner connection and inner guidance.

AMIR: You spoke, and of course it makes sense, about how the relationship between you and a student changes as the student progresses along the path. Are there aspects of the relationship that remain the same?

LLEWELLYN: The inner closeness with the teacher is a "closed circle of love" and remains the same. My sheikh said that, for the teacher, "The very beginning and the end are the same; it is a closed circle. For the disciple, of course, it is very different; he has to complete the whole circle. As the disciple progresses, he feels the Master nearer and nearer, as the time goes on. But the Master is not nearer; he was always near, only the disciple did not know it." This is from *Daughter of Fire*.

When I first meet someone who is drawn to follow this path, I feel the real nature of our spiritual connection and relationship of the soul. But it takes the student many years to come to know this inner connection, this quality of love and spiritual friendship.

AMIR: Have you had students who were on the path and at some point wandered off the path?

LLEWELLYN: Yes, of course, some students wander off the path, mainly through being caught in the illusions of the ego, or the world. I have also found that for the first years on the path, students often make mistakes, get caught in illusions in the outer and inner worlds, yet they can remain on the path. Yes, they need to learn from these mistakes, but it is just part of the journey. But as the path progresses and the wayfarer is given more and more access to their divine nature, they have to live more and more aligned with their highest nature. Then mistakes have more lasting consequences when, for example, an individual gets caught in a spiritual illusion, a spiritualized sense of self, or does not ground the path in outer service in everyday life, or gets caught in a negative relationship. There are so many different illusions that can attract us and the danger is that the illusion covers over the real light of the path, and the individual is drawn back into the ego.

AMIR: What happens then to the relationship between you and the student?

LLEWELLYN: If a wayfarer makes a serious mistake, or gradually turns away from the path, of course I feel a certain disappointment, particularly if a spiritual opportunity, an opportunity for the soul to grow and evolve, is missed. If the individual continues down this road, gradually they forget the path and the true nature of their inner connection with the teacher, and I am no longer able to reach them on the plane of the soul. It is very sad, probably one of the greatest sadnesses of being a teacher, because it is a sadness of the soul. But at the same time, I have to be detached; otherwise, I could try to influence the individual, and the person has to be left free. Love is about freedom. On this path, freedom is very important. It is a path of complete freedom.

AMIR: Did such disappointments change something in you?

LLEWELLYN: At the beginning, I was very naïve, but over the years I have learned about the many ways the ego can seduce us. Maybe I have grown more mature; but also a certain sadness remains, a certain loss of innocence.

Behind these questions and my answers there is another quality that belongs to this link of love between teacher and disciple, which I find difficult to fully articulate. This is a deep feeling of love and care, so that if the student is able to make the journey, there is a joy and happiness, balanced by the sadness and disappointment for those who are waylaid by the ego, by anger or a personal power drive, or many of the other obstacles to real surrender. Although I am detached, I also feel deeply for the spiritual well-being of those who are drawn to this path.

AMIR: What have you learned from your work with your students?

LLEWELLYN: I have learned about human beings and how the path works mysteriously within each of us. And I have marveled at the grace that is given, and how easy it is to miss the opportunities that are given, how easily the lower self and the illusions of the world cover and distort the inner light, the real guidance, and yet how we are helped again and again, despite our mistakes.

I have also learned how often the way I have approached the path with a certain ruthlessness and masculine drive is not necessarily appropriate for others. I have always pushed myself, but I have found for most people this is not the best way, that love and acceptance work better.

I also have discovered many of my own limitations, lack of understanding of certain human dynamics. For example, when I first started teaching, many women appeared to have issues with a lack of self-worth which I had never encountered before, and I had to try to learn about these issues, though I do not think I have been fully successful. Certain psychological dynamics I just do not understand.

AMIR: Do you need to be a teacher in order to continue learning and developing?

LLEWELLYN: I will be happy to pass on some of the responsibilities of being a teacher to the one who comes after me. Being a teacher is both a grace and a burden, especially in the West, where there is so little understanding of the true nature of this relationship. And, of course, there is a central part of my journey that has nothing to do with being a teacher, just a human being, a soul drawn towards the light. Just a piece of dust at the feet of my teacher.

AMIR: You feel this way even though you are a teacher yourself?

LLEWELLYN: In our tradition, the real relationship with the teacher is once and forever, from lifetime to lifetime. In my own experience, I could not live without the inner connection to my sheikh. I belong to him beyond life or death. Through his grace the journey continues.

SHAYKH FADHLALLA HAERI

My question about how the absolute-impersonal and the rela-tive-personal can be so closely—inseparably—related in the teach-er-student relationship appeared to be central for all of the Sufi masters and students I interviewed, including my exchange with Shaykh Fadhlalla Haeri, a Sufi master of Iraqi origin, who lives in South Africa and teaches worldwide.

AMIR: Do you have students for whom the personal relationship with you plays an important role in their journey?

FADHLALLA: Definitely, no doubt about it. There are some with whom I know the bond is exceptionally deep and strong, beyond any emotional relationship. It's beyond my ability to understand that bonding, but it is there. It's part of fate, and I take it as such. There are students who I don't hear from for months or years but that relation-ship is always there as though we never parted, there is no severance of the subtle inner emotional, mental and spiritual bond. It has to do with trust. Some people's trust in me is immovable, unshakable, unchangeable, total—which is why it has something sacred about it.

AMIR: Does such a relationship touch in some way the absolute dimension?

FADHLALLA: The soul, the mind and the body, each has its connect-edness. There are people with whom you feel great empathy and attraction on the mind level, and the same can be felt also on the body level. When you go to the soul, it's almost inexplicable. It's not an attraction of definable love or other measures of attraction. It's beyond description or even intuition. Such a connection opens the heart, that is why I say that trust is essential. It's inexplicable because it's not a trust in the cleverness or wisdom of the person, it is trust itself. I know it when it is there, and in most cases it remains and be-comes stronger as time goes by. The existential ups and downs have no effect on it. Such a person may have outer difficulties, a situation where you would have thought that the relationship would have to break down, and yet it was not touched whatsoever. That is because the connection is in another zone of consciousness.

AMIR: Can a relationship between two humans facilitate a relationship with that which is beyond human, with the absolute?

FADHLALLA: For sure. But these things happen in their own way, inadvertently. I don't think it's something that one can desire, expect or call for—it just happens. It resonates in the inner heart level, at the spiritual level. We don't know what beam of light hits where and how. You go into this zone which is no longer understandable by our limited and conditioned consciousness. These are the thrills of life, the mysteries of life.

SANIEL BONDER

Saniel Bonder, a former student of Adi Da and the founder of the Waking Down in Mutuality network, suggested in our interview an original view on the personal/impersonal paradox.

SANIEL: To me, there is a potential quality of the teacher-student connection that transcends the purveying of information, wisdom, energy and guidance that helps the student to attain realized autonomy. That quality of the connection has been strongly brought forth in the mystical dimensions of Christianity, as well as in the Vaishnavite or Krishna traditions in India, where the nature of the relationship isn't simply transactional, and it's also not a relationship between equals. It has to do with the dynamic tension between "the absolutely impersonal" and "the absolutely personal."

AMIR: Are you saying that the personal connection between teacher and student is an aspect of the absolute nature of this relationship?

SANIEL: Yes. A good example is that, for you and I, as we both acknowledged, clearly there has been a breakdown of something between us and our primary teacher, the one who contributed the most to our awakening and transformation, to whatever degree we're living it. Clearly something of that has ended and yet—that connection is very much alive! To me that indicates that there is an absolute dimension to the personal relationship, just as there is obviously the absolute, impersonal dimension of it.

AMIR: What does it mean, that there is an absolute dimension to the personal relationship?

SANIEL: It means that there is no place where the absolute stops and the personal starts. This non-difference is vitally profound for anybody who is doing anything like spiritual work in intense communion and connection with an "other," whether that other is one's student or one's teacher. Embodiment is the name of the game, and where the absolute meets the personal and suffuses it, it registers as a love beyond reckoning. It's a union. One of the ways I describe it is that it's not just that we're interconnected, we're inter-identified.

CHAPTER 4
SPIRITUAL INTIMACY
AND SEXUAL INTIMACY

Eroticism, covert or declared, fantasized or enacted, is inwoven in teaching, in the phenomenology of mastery and discipleship. This elemental fact has been trivialized by a fixation on sexual harassment. But it remains central. How could it be otherwise? Every "break-in" into the other, via persuasion or menace (fear is a great teacher) borders on, releases the erotic. Trust, offer and acceptance, have roots which are also sexual. Teaching and learning are informed by an otherwise inexpressible sexuality of the human soul.

—**GEORGE STEINER**, *LESSONS FROM THE MASTERS*

There is nothing more intimate to us, nothing deeper and more vulnerable, than our spirituality. This is where we experience our greatest passion and attraction. It is where we become most powerfully aroused, and it's where we can be most deeply violated. So it is profoundly erotic territory. And this expresses itself in our relationships to our teachers and students.

—**TERRY PATTEN** (FROM AN INTERVIEW)

In a committed spiritual teacher-student relationship, many people experience trust, love, intimacy and vulnerability at a depth and intensity the likes of which is rarely found in any other relationship. The student may allow the teacher to enter their "personal sphere" on many levels, emotional and physical included, to an extent rarely found even in romantic-sexual relationships. Nevertheless, most feel strongly that boundaries must be drawn in this relationship between spiritual and sexual love and intimacy. But why? In the context of such a relationship, why should the intimacy and love be kept within boundaries and not be allowed to include *all* aspects of human relationship, including the romantic-sexual?

MARIANA CAPLAN

Dr. Mariana Caplan—psychotherapist, yogi, and author of eight books in the fields of psychology and spirituality, as well as former disciple of American spiritual teacher in the Baul tradition, poet and rocker Lee Lozowick, for many years—has treated disillusioned and struggling students, former partners of spiritual teachers, done extensive psychotherapy with spiritual teachers working through challenging issues and written extensively on subjects related to controversial and challenging topics on the spiritual path, seemed to be the best person with whom to explore the question of why the teacher-student relationship should not include all aspects of the human relationship, specifically the romantic-sexual.

AMIR: I'd like to explore with you the distinction between spiritual intimacy and love and sexual-romantic intimacy and love. Where would you like to start?

MARIANA: I'd like to start with the mixture of psychological brokenness and spiritual longing that often make up both teacher and student. Many of us are psychologically wounded and traumatized—and nothing particularly bad has to happen in one's life for us to be traumatized—the everyday trauma of modern life impacts masses of people. This trauma opens us up and is often at least in part at the root of our attraction to the spiritual path. So in spiritual communities you find these wonderful, young, passionate, wounded warriors of Truth, who often do not have the most integrated personalities and psyches. And teachers are often in the same condition. A deeply wounded teacher can be powerfully transmitting knowledge and energy beyond themselves. To this you should add the very poor understanding of our psychological make-up that is common among teachers. Most teachers, even if they include some reference to psychological aspects in their teaching, merely give it lip service and have not pursued a deep understanding of this subject or their own therapy. When I hear spiritual teachers talk about psychology it's clear to me, having been a clinician for twenty-seven years, that they have very limited knowledge and understanding in psychology, which limits their understanding of both their own unconscious conditioning and patterns, as well as that of their students.

AMIR: Do you feel that sexual attraction can be a natural part of the teacher-student relationship?

MARIANA: In many cases, it can be. Many students experience love with their teacher, and spiritual love can look and feel just like sexual-romantic love but better, because it belongs to the domain of the divine. I place myself among the many people who made big mistakes in discounting and writing off very good human relationships because the flavor of that divine love affair was stronger than anything I knew. As a young woman, I hurt people and ultimately hurt myself, for example by sending my fiancée home so that I could be spiritually in love with a great yogi. It was a classic example of spiritual bypassing and the domain of psychological mistakes on the spiritual path that good people make and that I have been writing about my whole adult life. And usually one doesn't make these mistakes just once; most of us make them many times in different ways.

With my teacher, Lee, I fell deeply, spiritually in love with him, and although it was not an erotic love, it mimicked it in some ways. We used to talk about it amongst us in the community. Many people fall "in love" with their spiritual teachers in some form or another, but do not clearly understand the distinctions between spiritual love and romantic love. I recall some teachers saying that this "falling in love" is a very valuable part of the initial stages of relationship with a guru and that they didn't want to break that too soon because there was a lot of healing that can happen in that space. It's not just erotically falling in love, but it's hard to describe. I call it falling spiritually in love. Everything in your being—which may include your body and sexuality—is moved and touched. And often that's happening because we are being *seen*.

AMIR: What do you mean?

MARIANA: This was my experience with Lee. I felt that I was being seen in a way that I had never been seen. My whole life I had been told that I think too much and that I was crazy, and suddenly my spiritual yearning was respected and taken seriously by someone I respected. One of the first things that Lee said to me was, "If you become my student I'd expect you to act as an adult." I was twenty-five, barely an adult, but I felt that part of my essence was being seen.

So towards the one who sees that you feel tremendous love, and that love can have different elements to it. One day that person can feel like a father, the next day they can feel like a lover or a close friend, and sometimes it can feel like complete union, no separation. I would say that to feel in love with our teacher and to feel erotic longing towards them is not uncommon. And we can assume that it's probably not uncommon also on the side of the teachers.

AMIR: Considering this, how do you think sexual attraction between teacher and student should be handled?

MARIANA: I don't think there are any rules about it, but I'd like to quote something that Lama Palden Drolma, a Tibetan Buddhist teacher who is a friend of mine, said in a private conversation we had. I cannot quote her exactly, but she said something along the lines that in her dream world, when anybody enters the path, especially a woman, they would be told that at some point on their spiritual trajectory there is a very decent chance that their spiritual teacher—if he is a man—is going to come on to them sexually. She said, "I don't think that's right or wrong, but it's my wish that students would know that, be prepared for that moment, and explore very consciously what they plan to do when that happens."

AMIR: Is it really that predictable?

MARIANA: I can definitely think of exceptions. For example, someone I've been close to and who has guided me for many years, both while my teacher was alive and since his death, is the Sufi master Llewellyn Vaughan-Lee. He is a teacher with tremendous transmission, who radiates something so powerful, that people who feel his transmission and have a certain psychological make up might feel that they are falling in love with him; that they are falling in love with the teacher, rather than with what he transmits. But he has maintained clear and clean boundaries over the course of his life as a teacher. In a very real way he is much more interested in his relationship with the Divine, so for him, keeping the boundaries clear and clean is spontaneous and natural. People do project love and eroticism onto him, but because of his clarity there has never been anything scandalous or problematic in his community around that. Also this phenomenon happens far more frequently around male spiritual teachers. It is far rarer to hear about female spiritual teachers confusing their boundaries or acting inappropriate with their students—a point really worth inquiring about deeply. Also, there are fewer instances of this confusion when the teacher-student relationship is not in the context of the guru-disciple model, and where it is clearer that the teacher is sharing a specific body of knowledge or wisdom, rather than being a representation of the Divine in some way.

AMIR: Would you say that "keeping the boundaries clear and clean" has spiritual significance and value?

MARIANA: I am a trained psychologist, I've been doing that for over twenty years, and to me, the question of boundaries is a spiritual issue. It's one of those issues we want to be inquiring about throughout our lives. I say, let's let the question of boundaries be a living, lifelong integrated part of our spiritual path and life. It's not just a psychological issue, of healthy or unhealthy boundaries, it's a profound spiritual question.

I don't have a grand theory on the way it works. I do explore it all the time with clients and keep discovering new levels of its importance. I definitely don't imagine the ideal connection with a spiritual teacher to be when the boundaries completely go away. It can be an amazing *moment* when that happens, and for a few weeks of my life that temporarily happened, but it's an experience that comes and goes. Some people may be at that state more often than others, and some teachers have a specific ability to bring others into that experience, but as we know for sure, this does not necessarily translate to a mature integrated human transformation in life. For daily, integrated life, the existence of boundaries is necessary. So boundaries are there, you don't have to create them. There are boundaries between things. It is our task to examine those boundaries and make them healthy, and to continue to navigate that over time.

Another way of looking at it is that we have many levels of experience concurring at the same time. Even when we are immersed in the mystical or absolute level and have an experience of boundarylessness, at the same time there are boundaries in every aspect of the relative level. So you may be experiencing that you are merging with or sharing the same field with your teacher, and nonetheless you are two different people experiencing it and there are boundaries between you. We don't want to ignore this or pretend that this is not the case. It's completely real.

I would love for people to consider that this is a profound principle that needs to be deeply explored at all levels of our development, and pay attention to it, rather than assume that they already know what it means. It's similar to the question of embodiment—you are in a body; and what it means; how to tend to your body; and how consciousness is experienced within the body is an endlessly progressive, deepening process of discovery. I would also venture to say that, at different levels of spiritual development, you find that your relationship to others, including to your spiritual teacher, and your perception of your boundaries, can change and develop, which opens new possibilities for exploration and refinement.

AMIR: Has your experience of boundaries changed over the years in your work as a psychologist?

MARIANA: For sure. As a young clinician in the field of psychology, I never talked about the love I felt for clients. I did not know how to communicate that in a healthy way, nor do most therapists. Many younger and newer therapists are learning to establish boundaries and not take on all of what their clients are feeling so that they won't get emotionally exhausted and burn out. Then, over the years, as my boundaries became healthy and established in that setting, I consciously chose to soften it, make it more porous. I started sharing my love with clients. So as a mature therapist, I can do what I couldn't as a young therapist. I am capable of feeling more deeply, of sharing and even taking on their pain at a deeper level without getting overwhelmed. I'm letting them know that even though I can feel their pain and it's very healing, that I can hold it and that it is okay. Having said that, each client is different and the way I use my boundaries is different. Some clients come with so much trauma that I need to have stronger boundaries in order to be there for them but also protect myself. Others come to me mature and integrated, and I can ease my boundaries. My choices are based on the individual that I'm responding to. In the same way, ideally, a teacher would be looking at this young woman who is gazing at them googly-eyed and say, "Wow, I have to be very clear with her that nothing romantic is going to happen between us." Maybe with someone else the teacher can express love without causing confusion.

AMIR: Do you feel that, under the right conditions, a love affair between teacher and student may be part of their relationship?

MARIANA: This is something I chewed on for many years: Spiritual teachers are dedicating their whole lives, every bit of time and energy, to their community. Are we expecting them to go out to a bar or get online to find the person who they are going to have a romantic relationship with? It can be possible for an authentic love relationship to develop between teacher and student under the right circumstances, but this requires a great deal of diligence and maturity on both [person's] parts, and even under this circumstance it may or may not work. Obviously, the student has to be mature enough for that, and that's not what we usually see—usually it's an older teacher with a young, sexy model, twenty years younger than them, and most of those don't work. They cannot work.

So it doesn't strike me as wrong that a spiritual teacher would end up in a deep love affair or long-term partnership with a student. It's absolutely a risk, but I wouldn't say it's wrong across the board as many others do. There are exceptions.

I tried to explore this question with many of my interviewees, but regrettably (and quite understandably) very few of them were willing to openly discuss their experience with regards to this charged question. The following are excerpts from interviews with two teachers who were willing to do that: Mooji (Anthony Paul Moo-Young) (Chapter 8) and Llewellyn Vaughan-Lee (Chapter 3).

MOOJI

AMIR: Mooji, do you think there is place for sexuality within a teacher-student relationship?

MOOJI: We need to be careful about this. When working with spiritual seekers who are asked to contemplate and introspect into the real nature of the Self, deep personal tendencies can often be triggered. Seekers often experience strong waves and feelings of insecurities, doubts, mistrust and vulnerability. As dormant tendencies are exposed, students find themselves unexpectedly in the midst of uncontrollable emotions, feelings and urges because their minds are not as yet settled or established inside the Self. While in such turmoil, if the student is with a teacher who they trust, they may feel the teacher's presence is their rock. This trust must not be broken. The true teacher will protect his students until they cross to safe shore.

The teacher's pivotal role is to guide the student. Because the teacher is ahead of the game he or she will know that the student will, initially, experience states of neediness and insecurity. The genuine teacher will be with each student as they "walk through the valley of the shadows of death," a most important stage in their connection as master and disciple. Most seekers will lean upon the teacher for emotional and spiritual support. They may, in their desperateness, imagine they are falling in love with their teacher. The teacher must not exploit the student here by becoming a lover to them. This would be the most tragic scenario in any master-disciple relationship. The personal identity of the seeker is more familiar with going to that romantic place within, and this play is one of the tricks of the ego-identity as it fights for survival. It is in the teacher's hands to guide their students through these states, and therefore it is crucial that they have transcended their own sexual insecurities and desires and don't fall prey to these false opportunities that come in front of them. If not, they are not serving their students. A teacher may redirect that energy and say, "I know that love you are feeling, but I want to remind you that it's not a romantic love. It's a love you're feeling for God, actually. It is not a personal love."

AMIR: Can you imagine any scenario in which it would be appropriate for a teacher and student to be in a sexual relationship?

MOOJI: What must be avoided is exploitation—where someone is put in your care and you are exploiting their vulnerability by satisfying your sexual desires. That's what makes people feel sick. But if a master forms a relationship with one of his or her students—say, they genuinely fall in love and have a real relationship of trust, respect and mentorship—then, of course, there is a legitimate place for this.

AMIR: For many people, the idea of a sexual relationship between teacher and student seems scandalous and brings up strong emotions. How do you understand that?

MOOJI: Public perception does not always correspond with actuality. A teacher may fall in love with a student, and when looked at truthfully, the situation sometimes is not as scandalous as it's made out to be. It is just that in this role, a spiritual teacher is often placed under deep scrutiny and has to be "cleaner than clean" in the eyes of the world. Many religious-minded people throughout the world hold rigid concepts and expectations which they often project upon those they believe or presume to be spiritual teachers or spiritually awakened beings. But we should be careful before casting judgment so quickly, because we can't always rely on the human religious or social conditioning as a safe way of assessing things. You cannot always explain or grasp the deeper realities underlying human behavior. What we can say is that the actions of a genuine teacher would not intentionally hurt their students. True teachers don't take advantage of their students, they guide and protect and inspire them. This would be a key as to whether that relationship is founded upon truth or falsehood.

What society deems appropriate conduct for a spiritual teacher or master is heavily founded upon the worldly conditioning and perspective. Human beings are inconsistent in respect to their behavior. They generally have a tendency to be perfectionist in their thought but not necessarily in their actions. We tend to compare the worst in others with the best in ourselves. Thankfully, our salvation does not depend on human judgment but on the grace of the supreme Lord of the universe, whose wisdom is beyond the reach of the ordinary intellect of the worldly mind. This truth, directly grasped inside the heart is what makes life so incredibly miraculous.

LLEWELLYN VAUGHAN-LEE

LLEWELLYN: The teacher disciple relationship is the most intimate and yet impersonal relationship, because it belongs to the soul and not to the ego or personality. Unfortunately, in the West, because this relationship does not belong to our religious or spiritual tradition, as for example in the guru-disciple relationship in India, or the relationship with the Sufi sheikh, we have little context or cultural understanding of its subtleties, or the patterns of behavior that belong to this relationship. In Sufism, the correct behavior, or "etiquette" in relationship with the teacher is called *adab* and is central to the path.

Unfortunately, because the student often comes to this relationship with little or no understanding of this tradition, it is only too easy for him or her to project personal dynamics into this relationship—to see it only in personal terms. In Sufism, because this is a path of love and this relationship is founded upon love, it is only too easy for the student to mistake the soul love for physical or erotic love. And the fact that this soul love can have an inner erotic quality, as is expressed in many Sufi poems, only makes it more difficult. It is easy for the disciple to "fall in love" with the teacher, and to project the need for personal and physical intimacy into this relationship.

It is vital that the teacher is aware of these projections and does not become caught in the personal or sexual needs and desires of the student. The real relationship is from soul to soul, from heart to heart, and works at a much higher spiritual frequency than sexual desire, which is a lower chakra energy. The work of the teacher is to guide the soul of the disciple and to help free him or her from the illusions that belong to the world of the ego. It is therefore of great importance that the teacher does not respond in any way to sexual or personal projections, as this so easily corrupts the spiritual process, leading to issues of betrayal or abuse, which can damage the seeker and often hinder their spiritual aspirations for many years.

After teaching for over thirty years, I can say that I have experienced these projections, which are awakened by the unconditional love, acceptance and deep inner intimacy that is given in this relationship. And yet I have seen how the energy and practices of the path lead the disciple beyond these projections to realize the true nature of the soul relationship with the teacher, which can awaken a deeper and more enduring relationship with the divine. This inner relationship with the divine can, and often does, have an erotic element, but the experiences of divine intimacy, bliss, ecstasy and intoxication are far deeper and more intense than can come from any outer or physical relationship.

CHAPTER 5
PSYCHOLOGY AND SPIRITUALITY?

There is great debate, and in many cases a sharp divide, between practitioners of psychology and those of spirituality. On one end of the spectrum, most of mainstream psychology does not concern itself with issues of consciousness and spirit and rejects what is not scientifically quantifiable. On the other end, many contemporary spiritual traditions view the psyche as an unreal construct and believe that psychological work is an indulgent reinforcement of the story of the false self.

—**MARIANA CAPLAN**, "PSYCHOLOGY AND SPIRITUALITY: ONE PATH OR TWO?," FROM THE *HUFFINGTON POST*, SEPTEMBER 1, 2011

Psychotherapy is at the bottom a dialectical relationship between doctor and patient. It is an encounter, a discussion between two psychic wholes, in which knowledge is used only as a tool. The goal is transformation.

—**CARL JUNG**, IN THE FOREWORD TO SHENRYU SUZUKI'S *INTRODUCTION TO ZEN BUDDHISM*

Since I tend to freely use terms like "spiritual journey," "spiritual life" and "spiritual practice," I've been challenged many times with questions that, ultimately, boil down to one: How do you distinguish between the "psychological" and the "spiritual"? I often find that my attempts at clarifying this distinction fail to satisfy the person asking this question, especially if it turns out that an assumption, that the so-called "spiritual" is only a glorified and romanticized form of the psychological, underlies their question.

While working on and speaking with people about this book, I also encountered this question many times, in these two forms: "How do you distinguish between a 'psychological' and a 'spiritual' transaction?" and "What is the difference between the psychologist-patient and the spiritual teacher-student relationship?" Indeed, could the spiritual teacher-student transaction be essentially a unique type of the psychologist-patient transaction?

Take, for example, the following exchange I had with Dr. James Finley about his relationship with Thomas Merton: Was it a relationship between a spiritual master and seeker, based primarily on spiritual transmission, or did Merton function in James' case primarily as a psychotherapist, albeit an unconventional one?

JAMES FINLEY

AMIR: What led to your becoming a monk at the Abbey of Gethsemane and a student of Thomas Merton?

JAMES: My father was a very violent alcoholic and there was a lot of trauma, and my mother, who was Roman Catholic, taught me to pray for the strength to get through all the things that were happening. Then, when I was fourteen, in the Catholic school I was attending, someone started talking about monasteries and about Thomas Merton. I went to the school library and got his journal, *The Sign of Jonas.* I was deeply influenced by it. It gave me a sense that there is a place of refuge beyond suffering, and I felt that whoever wrote that book was well grounded in that. I kept reading it and was drawn to a point where I started writing to the monastery, saying that I wanted to enter the monastery and be a monk there. My goal was to sit at Merton's feet and let him guide me. As a kid, I saw him as the living embodiment of the mystical heritage of my own Christian faith.

AMIR: As a monk at the Abbey of Gethsemane, did you have a close personal relationship with Merton?

JAMES: This was a cloistered monastic order and we didn't talk to each other, but we used sign language to communicate. The idea was to be in solitude in community, seeking God together. It was a strict life of deep prayer and hard work. Thomas Merton was novice master, assigned to the task of spiritual formation of monks newly entering the monastery. So as a novice, I would see him once every other week for one-on-one spiritual direction.

I'll share a big moment I had with Merton. Because of the trauma I had experienced in my childhood, I would get anxious being around authority figures. When I started seeing Merton, my voice was shaking because I was so nervous being in his presence. He asked me what was going on, and I said I was scared.

Now this is so brilliant, this is compassion: I was just starting to work in the pig barn at the monastery, so he said, "Every day, before vespers, I want you to come in and tell me just one thing that happened in the barn that day." And so it was. I would come in, he would put aside his typewriter, and we'd start talking: I painted the fence, hurt my foot, fixed something broken, etcetera. He would remember all this, and it levelled the playing field for me.

I could talk about the deep longing for God that awoke in me when I read his books, but it's really true that of all I learned from those books, nothing was as deep as our talks about the pig barn. That's the teacher. That's a teacher meeting you where you're at and touching the hurting place with love, so it dissolves in love. To me, that's the essence of the teacher.

BARRY MAGID

With these questions in mind, I went to interview Zen teacher Barry Magid, a psychiatrist and psychoanalyst as well as the Dharma heir of Charlotte Joko Beck and founder of the Ordinary Mind Zendo in New York City. Barry has published numerous articles and books on the integration of psychoanalysis and Zen, including *Ordinary Mind: Exploring the Common Ground of Zen and Psychoanalysis* (Wisdom, 2002), in which he wrote:

> *"What is the relationship of a student to a Zen teacher? Is it analogous to that of a patient and a psychoanalyst? How central is this relationship to what happens in meditation? I have had psychoanalytic colleagues who, prizing the intimacy, mutuality, and relatedness they achieve over the years with their patients, assure me that the Zen student/teacher relationship must inevitably be distorted by issues of hierarchy and authority. They ask, 'What kind of freedom could anyone possibly find within such a rigidly formalized, hierarchical relationship?' Yet anyone who has had a long-standing student-teacher relationship can testify to the level of intimacy that is achieved. Superficially, of course, a Zen teacher takes a very different stance toward a student than an analyst toward a patient. The analyst's basic stance is one of engaged, personal inquiry; the Zen teacher's is one of challenge, if only the challenge of leaving everything alone. I've often joked that the quintessential analytic intervention is a curious and quizzical 'Really?' while the Zen teacher's quintessential response is 'So what!'"*

My interview with Barry took place at his clinic on Central Park West in New York City; afterwards, I asked him to refer me to a few of his students. He connected me with two of his Dharma heirs, Karen Terzano and Claire Slemmer, who were, respectively, a voiceover artist and an actor who is currently the director of the Ordinary Mind Zendo. The interview with Claire shed an interesting light on the psychological or spiritual question, as well as on the way in which the teacher's bias influences the student.

AMIR: How did you became both a Zen teacher and a psychotherapist? Did you start off with one and then added the other?

BARRY: I actually started reading books on meditation at the same time that I started reading on psychotherapy and psychoanalysis, so right from early on I was interested in how these two systems of personal transformation could shed light on each other. Originally, in the '50s, when people like Erich Fromm were studying Zen Buddhism, they did so because they were trying to use it as a way to pry open psychoanalysis and let in some fresh air. You see, when you encounter something like Zen, you realize that radical character transformation is possible that doesn't seem to be dependent on all the things that psychoanalysis depends on, so it opens a question of what is necessary and sufficient for a transformation, which I was very interested in.

Then, as you know, in my generation, there were many problems with Zen teachers, especially repeated sexual scandals, which begged the question of "How could these enlightened people behave in such a way?" Then, psychoanalysis had something to say about the unconscious parts that we have to come to terms with, and about dissociative processes with parts that were not engaged by spiritual practice. But when I started out, there was the idea of enlightenment experiences trickling down to your entire personality and transforming you spontaneously. This was supposed to make unnecessary all the psychological work, which Zen teachers of those days used to refer to the "merely psychological." There was this idea of a spiritual hierarchy, where sometimes you have to work down to that psychological level, but the real important level was the spiritual, at the top. I think that's a lot of nonsense.

AMIR: Why do you think that?

BARRY: To me, it's clear that all these transcendental fantasies are by and large born out of self-hate. People are unable to stand the mind and the body that they have, and they start on a lifelong quest to somehow climb out of their own skin and out of their own mind. They want to get rid of their vulnerability, their anger, their sexuality, their dependency, and they believe that through spirituality they are going to attain some kind of an invulnerable imperturbable state, where they can never be hurt again.

Another bad fantasy that is endemic to the spiritual community teachers who, to one degree or another, buy into it and collude with it, is that of the super human. You know, because *human* isn't working out so well. It's the projection of all goodness outside of oneself, which leaves the self empty but full of aspirations. It's a typical position that the person on the spiritual quest has, that "spiritual" is in some way "out there," and this position becomes part of unexamined and unresolved power dynamics of dominance and submission. What happens is that the student takes the position of "I cannot match myself to this ideal figure, but as long as I pay the price"—which is sometimes financial, sometimes sexual, sometimes just in terms of buying into a whole system—"at least I'm on my way."

So much of what I do in day-to-day practice is get the source of meaning and value out of the sky and back down to earth and to the person's everyday life. So, in that sense, I see myself and the practice as religious and not spiritual, which is contrary to what most people want to do these days.

AMIR: Don't you see any difference between the motivation of people who come to you to practice Zen and those who come for psychotherapy?

BARRY: As I said in an interview a couple of years ago, everybody comes to practice for the wrong reason. What I'm trying to do is make explicit something of the whole psychological agenda that people call "spiritual," which usually means becoming "more than ordinary." A lot of people come to the practice with a spiritual fantasy—of transcendence, specialness, autonomy, a longing to exist in a "higher" realm; the goal of practice is actually to help them get over it.

I'd say that for 99 percent of the people Zen practice is motivated by psychological issues. People come because they find life too complex and full of pain and strife and they're looking for a place that's utterly simple and free of pain. They come because they have a lot of difficulty accepting themselves as they are. Many of them are what I call "spiritual anorexics," who are trying to extirpate some part of themselves that's hateful and create an idealized perfected self. So people come mainly for these reasons and they want to use religious or spiritual practice to actualize these fantasies.

Did you know that Wittgenstein wanted his best students to go and become doctors and engineers? He saw philosophy as largely therapeutic and disentangling: you do philosophy to get over your philosophical confusion and preoccupations. You almost do it so that you'll finally get to the point of no longer doing it. For a lot of the people who come to practice Zen, if they can get over it, get married and have a good job, then the practice did its job. There are a very small number of people for whom a daily religious life is their calling, and settling into the lifetime of formal practice is natural and satisfying.

AMIR: So you don't see a distinction between what I'd call "therapeutic relationships" and "transformative relationships"?

BARRY: I don't believe in that distinction. It's a fiction. People on the so-called "transformative" side like to imagine they are doing something that is not psychological, but I won't go along with that.

AMIR: Don't you think that there is such a thing as spiritual aspiration, that doesn't come from a sense of there being something wrong?

BARRY: I don't think there is. You know, in my generation, when I started, there were a lot of people who were in pursuit of enlightenment, but we were pursuing it because we were unhappy, miserable people, and we were looking for relief from our suffering. I mean, there may be people who want to pursue the spiritual life for its own sake, for reasons that are not psychological, but I've never met them. Maybe you are one of them. It's people's personal issues that drive them. You do sometimes have people who spontaneously had an unusual experience when they were young and they're trying to make sense of it. They experience a big incongruity between that moment of wonder and the mundane life they're living, so they're trying to figure out how to put them together.

AMIR: Is there a difference in the role that the relationship with you plays between students who come to you as a Zen master and patients who come to you as a therapist?

BARRY: It's the same, just a different container. For most people, my approach is basically "What is the matter? What do you think is missing? What do you think is damaged? What is it that you have trouble leaving alone in yourself? Can we create a container for you to stay with the experience you ordinarily avoid?" It's the same business. Some people gravitate to this side or the other, but I don't think there's much difference.

I hope you get to meet a few of my students and ask them about my relationship to them. For example, one of them is a woman who had been a monk for some years before she met me, and she was very committed, very accomplished and very depressed. Because she had wanted to have nothing to do with anything psychological and emotional, and a vulnerable part of her was just stifled. Then she read my book and reached out to me, and we corresponded and eventually met, and my experience of this meeting was like I just had to add some water and she blossomed. It was very spontaneous. A similar thing happened with a few other people who came to me after being in some kind of a training situation for many years, where they had been left to endlessly chase a carrot—and I just rescued them from it.

AMIR: Do you feel that being a teacher and having students is something you need for your continued spiritual development, deepening and maturation?

BARRY: It's just what I do; I don't want to be unemployed.

AMIR: You wouldn't be—you would still have your practice as a psychotherapist.

BARRY: It's the same practice. It's one thing. It's how I exercise my talents and interests. I need my students in order to do it, like you can't play baseball by yourself. I need all these people in order to have the game. I don't really give any thought to my ongoing spiritual development, I don't give a damn about that really. I feel like I can try to become a little more patient and more understanding with people and less self-involved, but honestly I think I'm pretty much the way I'm going to be and I'm all right with it. I do what I do, I do it pretty well for the little group of people I do it with, and I hope to do it for another decade or so.

AMIR: I assume there is an element of transference—of love, admiration and idealization—in some of your students' relationship to you. How do you relate to it, or work with it?

BARRY: Transference, admiration and idealization are necessary and inevitable in a relationship like this, and over time it should mature into internalization of values and practice, so that ultimately we feel that we are doing the same thing together. I can see it in my relationship with my own teacher, Joko. Initially, I idealized her, but over time I internalized it as a practice and values, so it's not outside of me anymore. Ideally, that's what happens to students.

AMIR: One last question—how do you avoid those traps that many teachers have fallen into, that the students' idealizations create?

BARRY: Well, I think you must always be careful to the degree that your own self-esteem is dependent on the admiration and adoration of your students. For me, it's somewhat easier, because I'm not that charismatic... But it is very much the same thing that happens in the psychoanalyst's office, and we learn to handle it with a lot of training, of how to deal with people's needs for you, and just as importantly, your needs for them. It's important not to imagine that you are invulnerable or autonomous. It seems to me that the people who get in real trouble are those who have denied their personal needs, and then all of the sudden it erupts.

CLAIRE SLEMMER

CLAIRE: In my first exchange with Barry, he asked me: "Why are you here? Why do you practice meditation?" I said, "I want to know what's going on here, why I'm here and what this is all about. I want to know what it is underneath this playground that we play on called life." He said, "Okay, now, what's the real reason that you sit?" I said, "I'll have to get back to you on that." I thought about it and thought that the real reason I sit is to manage my emotions, because I was so emotional and just tossed around back and forth all the time by my emotions, mostly in connection with work and men. That's where we started out.

AMIR: If you look back now at that exchange and the two different answers you gave Barry, which of them was truer?

CLAIRE: I think both. I think he tends to think psychologically, everything is rooted in your childhood or in your upbringing, but I also think that certain people are prone to wonder what life is about, who have that question all their life. I think I'm one of those people.

So it was both. I wanted to know what life was about and I also needed to figure out how to live in a sane and happy way. He might say that even my interest in spirituality was also a result of my conditioning and experience in my childhood, which is also possible.

AMIR: Since you have students yourself, if a student came to you and gave the answers you gave Barry in your initial exchange, how would you respond? I'm asking because obviously in every tradition there are big variations between teachers depending on their life experience, personality, philosophical tendency etcetera, and although you are Barry's successor, it sounds like you have a somewhat different slant on things than he does.

CLAIRE: If a student came to me and said the same thing, I don't think I would ask him for the real reason. I think I would take his existential questions at face value, I would honor where he was coming from, and we would start our conversation there.

AMIR: Is it only where you'd start the conversation from, or do you think the whole way one goes about their life journey depends on that starting point?

CLAIRE: When I said I would honor the student's choice to start from his existential questions, it doesn't mean that my guidance of that student wouldn't later lead to psychological aspects. The existential and psychological aspects of the quest are completely intertwined. And I think the psychological path ultimately leads you to realize that there is no permanent self and that you're a part of something greater, interconnected and impermanent. It will lead to what you call "transformation."

In some interviews following those with Barry and Claire, I told the interviewees about Barry's assertion—that he saw no difference in the basic motivation between people who came to him for psychotherapy and those who came to practice Zen—and asked them if they felt the same with their students. When I interviewed Advaita teacher James Swartz, this was his response:

> *"Well, I would agree that everybody is motivated by one thing and one thing alone, and if this is what he means I would agree. Having said that, what is that one thing that everybody is motivated by? It's the desire to be free. So, a person who goes to seek psychological help wants to be free of what? Of subjective limitations. And a person that goes to Vedanta also wants to be free of subjective limitations.*
>
> *"The difference between Vedanta and psychotherapy is that we don't define the self as the person who thinks that he has those psychological limitations. We introduce him to a self beyond that self, to awareness itself, and that contextualizes the little person that they think they are, and then the psychological problem shrinks. And whilst in psychotherapy they can set you free of certain problems, they can't set you free of you. Because I just want to be free*

of me, me, my, mine, this person that I think I am. In psychother-
apy, they assume that that person is real and they want to fix that
person. So, that's the difference between Vedanta and psychology.
But it's true that the impulse of everybody is the same, and that is
to be free."

Barry Magid's and James Finley's two very different, even dia-
metrically opposed, perspectives on what spiritual awakening and
maturation are ultimately all about beg a question: Why do many
spiritual teachers emphasize the differences (or the one fundamental, all-inclusive difference) between their understanding, approach
and teaching and the understanding, approach and teaching of other teachers? What purposes does it serve, and what is sacrificed for
the sake of upholding those differences?

It is too easy to attribute the emphasis on differences to the "narcissism of small differences,"[1] but if we do that we may miss something important: that this practice may be necessary for the teacher
to play their role. For Barry and James, for example, their criticism of
other teachers and approaches serves well, and may be even essential, for what they are trying to do with people who come to them for
guidance. Barry wants them to let go of their dream of attaining an
"invulnerable imperturbable state" and engage themselves wholeheartedly in their ordinary daily life, and ridiculing their transcendental fantasies may be part of his teaching strategy; while James
wants them to realize freedom from attachment to or dependence
on objects, and emphasizing the difference between psychology's
goal to set you free of certain problems and Vedanta's goal to "set
you free of *you*" can be seen as a means to that purpose.

Considering that each path and teacher is unavoidably biased—
psychologically, culturally, philosophically and spiritually—and

1 "The narcissism of small differences" is a term coined by Sigmund Freud
in 1917 for his observation, that people and communities with much in
common and only minor differences between them are more hostile and
combative toward each other than those with major differences, often ex-
aggerating and ridiculing the "neighboring other's" qualities, because of
narcissistic hypersensitivity to details of differentiation.

that the bias is usually emphasized by the teacher, for the reasons described above and others, what is the effect of the bias on the students? Since what is medicine to one may be poison to another, how can the teacher's bias be of benefit to all their students? Can the teacher *see* the student and their psychological and spiritual needs through their bias? Can the student recognize the teacher's bias as bias, rather than take it as an ultimate, pure and undistorted view, and still benefit as much from the association with the teacher?

STEPHEN FULDER

We will leave these questions open, alive and inviting for ongoing observation and exploration, and end the chapter with the response I got from Vipassana teacher Stephen Fulder (Chapter 2) when I told him about my interview with Barry, and asked him what he thought of the motivation of people coming to practice with him.

STEPHEN: I would say it's up to me as a teacher to constantly take the motivation one step forward from wherever it is. Indeed, lots of people come to meditation at the beginning because they've got migraines or insomnia or things like that. I regard that as completely legitimate and I say, okay, let's practice. Then, as the practice continues, I encourage the discovery of deeper intentions, and refinement of the motivations.

When you climb a mountain, the reasons why you're climbing can change on the way up. Maybe, at bottom of the mountain, you say, "I'm going to climb that mountain because I have to cure my childhood issues. I had a terrible childhood, I have a lot of anxieties, and I need to climb this mountain and deal with them." I would respond, "Okay, let's start. I'll help you, we'll climb together."

We would start steadily climbing, and after a few hundred meters up the mountain I'd call out: "Hey, did you notice the small blue flowers next to the path?" "Yeah. They are really nice." I'd suggest, "Let's pay more attention to the flowers." Then, after another two hundred meters, I'd say: "What an amazing sunset." "Yes, it is really inspiring." After some time, I might throw out: "What about the flowers and the beautiful sunset inside you. Do you see them as you walk?" And you'd go: "Wow, oh, yes, of course, I have flowers in me…"

The whole psychological motivation that was at the beginning has really been purified and transformed. It becomes the longing for total freedom. Eventually that too dissolves, and there is no real need for any motivation based on the wish to be somewhere else other than where you really are and who you really are. The mountain vanishes and climbing is the same as being.

So as you progress, the motivation changes, and I work with that and encourage that change, so that with the deep experiences, a deeper and subtler motivation arises, and eventually needs to be let go of.

CHAPTER 6
TRANSFORMATIVE VS. TRANSLATIVE

There are several different ways that we can state the[se] two important functions of religion. The first function—that of creating meaning for the self—is a type of horizontal movement; the second function—that of transcending the self—is a type of vertical movement (higher or deeper, depending on your metaphor). The first I have named "translation," the second, "transformation."

With translation, the self is simply given a new way to think or feel about reality. The self is given a new belief—perhaps holistic instead of atomistic, perhaps forgiveness instead of blame, perhaps relational instead of analytic. The self then learns to translate its world and its being in the terms of this new belief or new language or new paradigm, and this new and enchanting translation acts, at least temporarily, to alleviate or diminish the terror inherent in the heart of the separate self.

But with transformation, the very process of translation itself is challenged, witnessed, undermined and eventually dismantled. With typical translation, the self (or subject) is given a new way to think about the world (or objects); but with radical transformation, the self itself is inquired into, looked into, grabbed by its throat and literally throttled to death.

—KEN WILBER, *ONE TASTE*

By its very nature, mysticism involves the danger of an uncontrolled and uncontrollable deviation from traditional authority. This is no doubt one of the many reasons for the widespread belief that a mystic requires a spiritual guide, or guru, as he is called in India. On the face of it, the function of the guru is primarily psychological. He prevents the student who sets out to explore the world of mysticism from straying off into dangerous situations. For confusion or even madness lurk in wait: the path of the mystic is beset by perils; it borders on abysses of consciousness and demands a sure and measured step. The Yogis, the Sufis, and the Kabbalists, no less than the manuals of Catholic mysticism, stress the need for a spiritual guide, without whom the mystic runs the risk of losing himself in the wilderness of mystical adventure. The guide should be capable of preserving the proper balance in the mystic's mind. He alone is familiar with the practical applications of the various doctrines, which cannot be learned from books. And he has an additional function, which has been very little discussed but is nevertheless of great importance: he represents traditional religious authority. He molds the mystic's interpretation of his experience, guiding it into channels that are acceptable to established authority. How does he accomplish this? By preparing his student for what he may expect along the way and at the goal. He provides at the outset the traditional coloration which the mystical experience, however amorphous, will assume in the consciousness of the novice.

—GERSHOM SCHOLEM, *ON THE KABBALAH AND ITS SYMBOLISM*

Before I interviewed Vedanta teacher James Swartz, I wanted to get a basic sense of the man—for whom I had received excellent recommendations from a few friends who attended his talks and retreats—and his teaching. In a few video clips, I saw him sitting next to an elaborate drawing, showing the relationships between the Five Elements—the Gross, Subtle and Causal Bodies, the three Gunas, Self and Awareness—which he kept referring to while teaching. Then, among his latest books, I found the *Yoga of the Three Energies*, whose book cover description claims that it provides "a sophisticated set of simple principles that allows anyone to eliminate negative emotions and transform the mind into a powerful tool capable of scaling the sacred heights of self-realization." But James' website, ShiningWorld.com, says that he teaches "traditional Vedanta in a non-traditional format," and that Vedanta is "not a religion, belief system, philosophy or a school of thought; it is revealed truth and is to be realized and understood as such. So there is never an argument."

I found all of this quite confusing. The chart and book description suggest a teacher and a teaching style that could be characterized as traditional, exoteric or "translative," while the statements on James' website suggest a nontraditional, esoteric or "transformative" teacher and teaching style, which, according to transpersonal psychologist and writer Ken Wilber, are suitable when "no new beliefs, no new paradigm, no new myths, no new ideas... not a new belief for the self, but the transcendence of the self altogether, is the only path that avails."

So which of these claims is actually true of James? What kind of teacher is he? With these principle questions in mind, I approached my interview with him.

JAMES SWARTZ

AMIR: I'm interested to hear how you see the relationship between the goal and the teaching model in your path—how the teaching model supports that goal.

JAMES: That's a very important question, because in Vedanta our definition of enlightenment is basically different from everybody else's, and the way we're going to teach is different from everybody else. You see, the goal is freedom from limitation, freedom from attachment to or dependence on objects. Everybody is trying to get rid of some sense of human limitation, from this feeling of lack or incompleteness, and Vedanta says that you can't achieve freedom by doing anything because you're already free. So, we—meaning, the teachers in this tradition—are not obligated to produce some kind of experience for the student. All we have to do is remove ignorance from the student, or better put it this way: we have to show the student how to remove their own ignorance. We can't do it for them, but we can give them a method that will allow them to understand what ignorance is and what knowledge is, and to remove their ignorance and to value the knowledge that they have.

Ignorance is a very tricky thing. It's hard-wired, and it basically comes in the form of dualistic thinking, based upon a false perception or understanding of the nature of reality. So we have to remove that sense of duality from them, or give them a way to remove that sense of duality; and that involves using certain teaching methods. It's a very technical business. How we teach is completely determined by our tradition, by the means of knowledge, which is what Vedanta is. It's not a philosophy, it's not a spiritual path or anything like that, it's just the means of knowledge. Means of knowledge is something that takes away ignorance. Vedanta takes away your ignorance about who you are and the nature of reality and what it is.

You see, I'm not teaching *my* stuff, and I'm not relating to the person's stuff. Vedanta doesn't actually address the person but the self—the free self in the person. The teaching actually defies the ego and goes directly to the self, which is why it's a method of revelation. But for that to work, there are certain qualifications that have to take place. The reason very few people understand Vedanta is because very few people are qualified to be taught.

AMIR: If it's all about knowledge, and it's understanding that liberates the individual, why do people need the contact with you? Can't they just read your book or watch your videos?

JAMES: No, you can't just read the book because if you don't know who you are, you're going to interpret the words incorrectly; your ignorance will interpret the words. We have to establish definitions, we have to see that the words are defined properly and the words have to be communicated in dialogue between teacher and student. So I've got to show you how to understand the words because the words in essence tell you that you're not the person that you think you are, and they help distinguish erroneous knowledge from correct knowledge. But the student doesn't know the difference between knowledge and ignorance—they often take ignorance to be knowledge.

AMIR: In addition to teaching knowledge and understanding, does the Vedanta teacher also teach by example?

JAMES: You have to live the teaching, you have to be free and you have to follow it for this to work. You know, if I'm chasing money, if I'm chasing the ladies, if I'm cutting corners in my private life and I'm telling you all this stuff and acting like a guru, how is that going to work for you?

AMIR: So do you think that one of the reasons people come to study with you and not just watch videos or read your book is because it's important for them to watch you and see that you are actually an example of where the path is leading to?

JAMES: That's right! Absolutely! You know, I searched for four years before I found my teacher, Swami Chinmayananda. I had plenty of experiences, but when I saw it actually embodied in this person, I immediately knew that that person was free. I still made a few tests, to check, and he passed the tests with flying colors; and then I knew it really was possible, it wasn't just talk. When you meet such a person, you know they're free. You see that they're compassionate, they're nonattached, they're clear and logical and make sense, and it's obvious to you that the teaching has worked out to set them free. When you see those qualities operating in them, it inspires you to apply yourself to that method of enquiry, to do the work. Your desire to be free just goes exponential. It skyrockets.

So when I met my teacher, I started talking about my spiritual experiences. He listened quietly for about five minutes, and then he said: "Listen, to be honest, we're not interested in your experiences. In fact, any experiences you've got you should put down and then shut up, pay attention and we'll get you out of here as soon as possible, because you're using a valuable real estate that others could use." That was it, and that was great! I thought: "Okay, fair enough—I don't want just to sit around!" I mean, I loved the guru, he was just a great guy, it was really fun being with him, but I didn't want just to sit there forever, I wanted to get on with my life, you know.

AMIR: In responding to people who write to you or ask you about their practice, etc., do you feel that you have developed certain skills that help you understand where they're at, what they're really asking, what they need?

JAMES: Teaching is very difficult because you have to figure out what the specific doubt is, so you can't just give them a generic answer. Ignorance is very clever and it formulates itself in a lot of different ways, so a good teacher has to listen very carefully. And this is a skill that you have to develop. And then you have to look at what they're saying in light of the teaching, and tailor the teaching to their question. That's a tricky thing to do. We're not like the Neo-Advaita people, who just say, "Oh, it's awareness," and just get it. That doesn't work. We have to give you an understanding that will allow you to go there, and if you're not clear, we have to teach you how to enquire and how to ask the right questions. There are a lot of questions we don't want to waste our time on, because they are the wrong questions.

AMIR: Is being a teacher part of your process?

JAMES: The answer is no.

AMIR: I understand why you say that, but do you feel that through the years that you have been teaching you [have] developed, maybe not in your understanding of the awakened state, but [in your understanding] of the human condition and of how to help people?

JAMES: Yes, I definitely improved as a teacher. I'm still evolving, in terms of presenting this. I mean, I was okay when I started and I'm very good now. I mean, I can sell ice to an Eskimo, but when you communicate, you have to figure out where the other person is at, and you've got to help them where they're at, and I'm constantly getting better at that. And I'm constantly refining the way I put together teachings, so that now I'm able to come at it in a lot of different ways, whereas before I only had a few points of access. So now I can reveal the complexity and beauty of the teaching and inspire people in that way. Because when you really understand what Vedanta is, it blows your mind. There's nothing like it out there.

AMIR: Are there people for whom you feel that you personally played an important role in their awakening, that maybe you giving them the right advice or hitting the right spot at the right moment did the trick?

JAMES: Sure, but in general we don't give advice. We do make suggestions, and we make them quite subtle, and if a person is quite sensitive, he'll pick up on them. People do ask me directly for advice on certain things, but I'm very hesitant to give advice, because Vedanta is not personal. We're not really teaching individuals; everybody is the same person. The idea that you're special, that you're an individual with your problems—we don't accept that concept. We're just teaching the human being, not a specific person. So I can relate to you as a specific person with a history, nationality, religion, birthplace, mother and father, or I can relate to you as a human being. Ignorance is the same for everybody—young and old, rich and poor, Muslim or Jew—who cares, it's all the same.

Based on my observations and his admissions, James is working entirely within the boundaries of language, concepts and rational thinking; hence he is a "translative" teacher. His effect on his students, on the other hand, reportedly takes them out of the realm of language and rational thinking and into the realm of the ineffable and the paradoxical—hence he is "transformative." So which *is* he, a translative or a transformative teacher? Or both?

One way of solving this question is suggested by the Buddhist Shurangama Sutra, which tells us: "The Buddha told Ánanda, 'You and others like you still listen to the Dharma with the conditioned mind, and so the Dharma becomes conditioned as well, and you do not obtain the Dharma-nature. This is similar to a person pointing his finger at the moon to show it to someone else. Guided by the finger, the other person should see the moon. If he looks at the finger instead and mistakes it for the moon, he loses not only the moon but the finger also. Why, because he mistakes the pointing finger for the bright moon.'"

At first glance, the finger-and-moon metaphor seems to suggest the right relationship between the translative teacher's finger and the transformative moon. But upon closer observation, I find it misleading. In reality, just as much as the goal determines the direction in which the teacher points their finger, the direction in which the teacher points their finger determines the goal. The teacher and the goal relationship is unlike the finger and the moon but like the Ouroboros, the serpent eating its tail. Indeed, who can tell where the finger ends and the moon begins?

I wonder if the reason that the translative-transformative distinction does not seem to always work in reality as well as it does on paper, is that what makes the difference between a translative teaching and a transformative one is not necessarily the *teaching* per se but the *teacher-student connection*. That is, the same words, the same concepts, even the teacher's same voice and gestures, can provide a translative framework to one student yet have a transformative effect on the student sitting next to them. For a similar reason, to an outside observer of a teaching situation, the teacher may seem like they are delivering a translative teaching, while for at least some of the students, the experience is of a transformative transmission.

CHAPTER 7
THE TRUST CONTACT

The devotee's ongoing gesture of voluntary submission signals to the teacher that he or she can feel free to engage the disciple in what can be called the "game of enlightenment." The rules of the game state that the teacher is invested with the authority and power to make spiritual demands on the disciple and, if necessary, to reprimand and discipline the student.

—**GEORG FEUERSTEIN**, *HOLY MADNESS*

To remain trusting of [my teachers] was perhaps the greatest thing I learned, not because they turned out to be perfect and all-wise, but because I came to realize that trust was my practice and my responsibility, not theirs.

—**NORMAN FISCHER**, *THE TEACHER IN THE WEST*

I believe one can't have faith without a degree of doubt... If you have faith without doubt, you are liable to become trapped in a closed belief system. If you have doubt without faith, then you risk slipping into a kind of nihilistic skepticism. Somehow one needs to hold the two.

—**STEPHEN BATCHELOR**, "THE TWINS: FAITH AND DOUBT"

DIANE MUSHO HAMILTON

I was introduced to group facilitator and Integral Spirituality and Zen teacher Diane Musho Hamilton during her visit to Israel in 2011, and I interviewed her on the topic of teacher-student and group-individual dynamics. That interview took place only a few months after Diane's own teacher, Genpo Merzel Roshi, stepped down from his teaching position after admitting to several extra-marital affairs. I wanted to explore with her the question of trust in the teacher-student relationship.

AMIR: How did you meet your teacher? Were you looking for a teacher at the time?

DIANE: Yes. It was really based on that. I knew that I wanted to deepen my meditative discipline and I wanted to do it in relationship with a master. It was that choice—it wasn't simply that I wanted to practice or meditate. I wanted that direct—in our tradition, we say "mind to mind" and "eyeball to eyeball"—transmission with a recognized master. When I met Genpo Roshi and he was teaching in the Zen tradition, I switched from what was predominantly Tibetan Buddhism to Zen at that point, for that very reason.

AMIR: That's interesting, because a lot of people run into their teacher not really looking for a teacher, but for you that was different, you very deliberately were interested in the relationship with a teacher. Why, what did you think was so important in that relationship?

DIANE: I started the practice of Buddha Dharma when I was twenty-two. I went to Naropa Institute and studied there until I was twenty-six, and then I did different retreats, I went to Asia, spent some time with a Tibetan master, came back and then had my son. So by the time I decided to go deeper, when I was in my mid-thirties, I'd seen that in a self-designed practice there was simply a limit to what you can experience, that if you don't study with a master you probably won't be able to go as far. The mind-to-mind transmission experience, that's something you can only get from a realized master. And the part of us that needs to be shaped and molded in order to embody and manifest that realization, that also gets shaped in the relationship to the teacher.

AMIR: What does the transmission mean to you? How does it work?

DIANE: We're habituated to our conventional conditioned mind, so to have an experience of nonduality of the unconditioned, vast, open quality of mind, you literally have to swim in that water with someone who has that experience in an ongoing fashion. When you're in the company of a spiritual master, they convey that experience through their being, so in Zen, we talk about becoming one with the mind of the master. Becoming one with the heart and the mind of the master can only be done by being in their presence, by sitting with them. That's what makes it possible for us to move beyond the limited space into that vast open, unconditioned space.

AMIR: Now that you're a teacher, I assume that your experience is that most of the time your state of consciousness is quite ordinary, that you're not in an enlightened state 24/7.

Maybe some rare individuals are enlightened all the time, but it seems to me that in most teachers something gets activated when they're in their role as a teacher, in the relationship with their students. If that's true, it means that when we meet our teachers and interact with them, they are in a specific state of mind that has to do with their interaction with us as students. In other words, it means that the teacher's state is a more relational than usually thought of and described, and that being in a teacher role should help the teacher maintain their clarity, focus, attention, care and all those qualities that we associate with a higher consciousness or higher spiritual state.

DIANE: Let me analogize with being a group facilitator, which I spend a lot of time doing. One of the challenges I have in teaching my students how to be group facilitators is that awareness tends to be limited a lot of times. They'll focus on what one person said, or on the dynamic between two people, but as a facilitator, you always have to keep your awareness extended, you have to be aware of the entire situation in every moment, because what's happening to the whole is really what it is. So when I'm facilitating, because I'm being watched, I'm held right on point to that, but if I'm in a casual situation and I'm not being watched, then it's easy for me to collapse my awareness and to get focused on this little pesky issue, or that irritating thing, and I do indulge that quite a bit; but I can't indulge in a situation when I'm being observed. So, I think the point you made is a good one, that the student asks the teacher to be all of who they are and more, and that's a good thing.

AMIR: Would you say that when you're in front of a big group of students, functioning as a teacher, then the personal relationship doesn't play such an important role?

DIANE: Then the personal relationship is placed within the larger context. For instance, a student can raise their hand at a pesky issue and you know that interacting with that individual will actually be affecting the whole room. I noticed that if I'm in a room with 300 people, I'm so much more precise in how I interact with that student, while sometimes in one-to-one situations I just let the sloppiest exchanges happen, because I'm not held to that kind of precision.

AMIR: That's fascinating. Can we say that when you speak to a group of students it brings out certain human qualities in you, but also that when you speak with somebody where there is personal chemistry or love with that person, it brings out other qualities in you, of care and compassion, that might also bring out a different response in you and have a different effect on that person?

DIANE: I think it's true, and it's also true that the more intimate we are, the closer and more loving we are, there's more capacity for us to challenge each other. It's like the greater the love the greater the challenge, and the greater the potential. I'm at my best with the people I'm closest to, but sometimes I'm at my worst. But there is potential in that worseness...

AMIR: Yes, because you care about each other, so it challenges you more than if it was just somebody who comes and goes.

DIANE: Yes, that's right. There's a depth and a kind of inescapability from the commitment, and we know that life is our opportunity and that it is so precious, so why waste it?

AMIR: I think what is also difficult to understand is that there is an element in the teacher-student relationship which is beyond time. I see this in my relationship with Andrew. I feel that on a certain level, *something* wouldn't change in my relationship with him even if I discovered he was a mass murderer. Which makes it very disorienting, because it is a relationship that happens in time and changes over time *and* it is also a relationship beyond time and beyond anything that happens in time.

DIANE: What you say is absolutely true. I'm estranged from my teacher and I feel the same way. I feel that we have a connection beyond space and time, and it's not anything I question. Whether he and I would ever engage one another there is a question for me, and how to do that is another. And yet I feel that I'm still being taught by him through our separation.

AMIR: How do you understand that?

DIANE: I don't. Because as soon as we enter into nonduality, our relationship with space and time changes and the relative conventions of self and other are challenged. In a certain way, we just have to recognize it and leave it at that. That's why I love the mystic poets, because they express what is difficult to express in words. You probably know the poem by Hafiz, where he says: "The Truth has shared so much of itself with me that I can no longer call myself a man, a woman, an angel or even a pure soul. Love has befriended me so completely it has turned to ash and freed me of every concept and image my mind has ever known."

AMIR: What we are talking about now seems unique to the teacher-student relationship, because it's a relationship between individuals and yet it's beyond individuality. I don't experience it in other relationships.

DIANE: No, me neither. There are some friendships, like you and I are tasting at this moment together.

AMIR: We get a taste of it, that's true, but it's as if something is forged or etched in your soul in the relationship with the teacher, and there is nothing you can do about it.

DIANE: No. I remember meeting one of Andrew's students who had a bit of a grudge and was complaining about his experience, and I said, "I hear what you're saying, but you need to know that whatever you did practice there, I feel it in you." As you say, there is something that's etched in you, and I felt in him that quality. First of all, it's that training of attention that goes on when you're in the company of a master, of your capacity to listen. Then it's your willingness to yield your perspective for a larger one, or different one. There are all kinds of traits that come along with your ability to quiet your mind in order to receive the teacher's guidance. It's like all those things get cultivated in the ongoing relationship with the master or teacher, and they become deep habits.

AMIR: One of the things Andrew said in my last interview with him was that we—his older students—were all practicing Guru Yoga in the relationship with him, that it was our main practice. To me, Guru Yoga is what you're talking about, and it's very rare to really want to tune in and pay deep attention to another person, to see things through their eyes. It's rare that we want to make such an effort.

DIANE: Absolutely. That's what the discipline of being in a relationship with a guru or master is, to be willing to train your attention on them. For me, I'm humbler in a certain way around my Zen practice, but when I'm facilitating I really make that demand on my students. I want them to follow what I'm seeing. We can talk about it, but we're not going to negotiate it, because we have an agreement that they're there to absorb my way of seeing. So I don't want to debate about what I'm seeing. I'm happy to explore it, but I'm going to prevail, because I'm in the hierarchical position.

How often are we willing to put ourselves in hierarchy in order to be able to see what someone else sees? We don't struggle as much around other relationships, but because the relationship with the teacher involves our heart, because it's unknown and because it's our consideration of ultimate meaning, we do challenge ourselves around it. And we should.

AMIR: The thing about that is that you have to renounce quite a bit of your discrimination and ignore your doubts, in order to benefit from this kind of transaction. On the one hand, there is need for deep trust and surrender, and on the other, you want to cultivate open-eyed, critical thinking, and these two elements, which are essential for human growth and maturation, seem to contradict, to clash. How do you work with that?

DIANE: What do you do when you have a discrimination that you think is actually important for the community? Or even more importantly, what happens when you feel that the teaching method is endangering people? How do you ethically work with that? I think that's exactly the question we should be living. There is not an easy answer, and both teachers and students have to work with how to navigate that potential collision.

Sometimes I say to my students, "When it comes to your wellbeing, your growth, you and I can have any kind of back and forth you want, but there's probably going to be a moment—if we're talking about you—that I'm going to pull rank. Because that's what you've asked me to do. If you're talking about the Sangha, or the organization, even if you're talking about my interaction with another student, I'd be interested to hear what you have to say and take it in, just like any piece of feedback. Perhaps I will agree and perhaps I won't, depending on whether it resonates with me. But when it comes to you, I will pull rank, because that's precisely our agreement. We know that the ego will always move toward self-protection, so in relation to you as a student, you're going to find a lot of reasons to disagree with my feedback." So, in that very specific way, the hierarchy needs to be maintained.

AMIR: Since, as we know, a teacher can be very evolved along one line and quite underdeveloped in others, we also have to take into account the possibility that giving the teacher such a mandate may well lead to disappointment or worse.

DIANE: I think the aspiration for spiritual evolution, joined to a very real sense of disappointment, is probably the place I like my students to be.

AMIR: Please say more about that.

DIANE: The aspiration opens up the territory and the disappointment grounds it. Evolution is a very slow and messy thing. You know, Trungpa Rinpoche always said enlightenment is the ego's greatest disappointment. Students bring a tremendous amount of idealism. I want that idealism to be joined with a very real sense of the fallibility of each of us, of who we are. Human is that position between heaven and earth. It's not simply the God realm, it's actually that in-between place that integrates everything that's bent, sluggish, painful, deluded. The heart is an integrative function. It's one of the agreements I make with people, that they have to be willing to be honest with me, to talk with me about their issues—and they have to be willing to confront disappointment, not just in me but in themselves.

AMIR: As a teacher, you really are pulling on those two ends, because you also have to inspire them not to give up.

DIANE: Absolutely. I want them to experience expansiveness, freedom, compassion, an opportunity to love that is real, but not by making it easy, and not by fulfilling their fantasies of whatever their spiritual Shangri-Las are like. It's a ruthless situation. Facing the degradation, the violence in the world, the injustice and the suffering, as one person put it, the very awkward moment between birth and death. It's something damn right awkward about being a human being. I think I'm more of an integrative teacher. If you look at my students and the people who work with me, they actually come to me for that purpose. Integrating the awkwardness of being human feels very important to me.

AMIR: I guess the ideal state is when the aspiration for enlightenment and the acceptance, even the painful acceptance, of our humanity are no longer in conflict.

DIANE: Yes, exactly. As we say in Zen, enlightenment is delusion, delusion is enlightenment.

One of my strongest impressions of Andrew Cohen in the first few days of our relationship was that he was a person I could deeply trust, and that shocked me. It shocked me because I realized that, up to that point, I had never met anybody who I felt was completely trustworthy; even more significantly, I realized that I also did not consider myself to be completely trustworthy.

What made Andrew so trustworthy to me was his unwavering commitment to that ungraspable part in himself, in me and in every human being that is absolutely trustworthy. The discovery of that trust in Andrew was simultaneously the discovery of that part in myself, and the bedrock on which my relationship with him was built. Indeed, many would attest that a relationship with a spiritual teacher can be a rare opportunity for the student to discover profound trust, initially in the teacher but ultimately in oneself and in life or existence itself.

The preciousness of trust, its deeply soul-healing effect and the many gifts that become available when one is willing and able to extend it, was one of the recurring themes in many of the interviews I conducted. The following are two excerpts on this topic: the first is from an interview with Bill Epperly, a transformational coach and teacher-student in Trillium Awakening from Chicago, and the second is from an interview with Aliya Haeri, a psychologist and spiritual counsellor and the wife of Sufi teacher Shaykh Fadhlalla Haeri, residing in South Africa.

BILL EPPERLY

AMIR: Would you say that the act of trust itself, even if you discover later on that whatever you trusted wasn't trustworthy, has a spiritual value by itself?

BILL: I think so, yes. There has to be openness to newness and transformation. In the spiritual world, there is something to be said for picking the best teachers and doing all we can to move forward in the positive direction. But I think this is a messy thing, and it's impossible to just sit at home and have FedEx deliver only the very best teachings. This is an unreal expectation; this is falling short of our vow to engage fearlessly with the world, seeking interaction, offering up all the results of our actions to our ongoing evolution and growth. Otherwise, after being burned, after your first girlfriend dumps you, why would you ever go through that again? Love doesn't care. Love calls us to go out and fall in love again and maybe get dumped by the second girlfriend—it's all part of the maturation process.

I think that a positive projection can be part of a mechanism that allows us to open up and to see our own enlightened self, or our best self, projected on the other. That can be very helpful to see ourselves in the other, and in time, if the relationship is strong and healthy, it will mature and the projection will change and slowly dissolve. We will come to re-own our projection and integrate it. If we'd been able to integrate our "Golden Shadow" [Jung's term for the positive, repressed parts of our self, which need to be integrated if the individuation process is to proceed] earlier on, we would have, but it takes time. We have to go through a maturation process.

ALIYA HAERI

ALIYA: I consider it a privilege and a gift to have a teacher in my life. Having a teacher is having in your life a mirror reflecting back to you higher consciousness. And it's your responsibility as a student to honor that transaction, first of all by relinquishing your worldview and to commit that, for the duration of your connection with your teacher, you would be as wide open as possible, suspend your conditioning and personal beliefs and really listen from a deep place beyond judgment and beyond defensiveness. It is a journey of trust, because we don't know what the outcome will be.

I think it's essential, if one is going to make a commitment to grow and evolve in one's higher self, to give that trust over to the teacher. Otherwise there is no end to the kind of picking and choosing what you like, which keeps you in the conditioned self, that only cares about what pleases and acknowledges you as an individual, while the entire journey is of departing from that conditioning and connecting with the place of pure consciousness.

The problem is, of course, that trusting the teacher is not always a good idea, and many people who made such a leap ended up feeling that it was a very regrettable choice. Surely it is wise, appropriate and beneficial for the student to deeply trust a teacher who is awake, competent and compassionate, but what to do when that is not or is no longer the case?

THOMAS STEININGER

After my interview with Diane Hamilton, I explored this question with Thomas Steininger, the German founder of the magazine *Evolve*, and my friend from Andrew Cohen's community.

AMIR: When I interviewed Diane Hamilton, she said that she encouraged her students to question her about the Sangha, the organization, the way she responded to other students, whatever they felt needed questioning, but when it came to them, when she challenged them on something and they disagreed, she "pulled rank." Otherwise, she said, the ego would always move toward self-protection, and the student would remain stuck.

THOMAS: I think what she's saying is very wise. This, I think has to be brought in the teacher-student relationship as a working assumption, or a working agreement. Not because she is the teacher and therefore she's always right, of course she can make mistakes, but because for the teacher-student relationship to work it has to be based on this working assumption. Not that this is necessarily always true, and it has to be renegotiated, but I would say that, as a whole, you either reject the teacher or you take him fully, but you don't take a negotiating relationship to the teacher. If this trust is not there, you basically put your own ego in charge immediately.

In my relationship with Andrew, I always had difficulties with certain aspects of his behavior, but I made a conscious choice to put it in the context of trust. I was even willing to go with him in the wrong direction at times, as long as the overall trust holds. This is more productive to do than negotiating the relationship. But at the same time, we don't want to assume that the teacher is incapable of making mistakes. We can't go there because if you hand over your responsibility to someone else you become dependent. It doesn't mean we do not surrender, but we surrender out of full responsibility. Such a position is much more difficult.

AMIR: Are you saying that there is greater value in assuming that the teacher knows what they are doing even if they are wrong, then get into negotiations with them?

THOMAS: For this to work, you have to establish a huge trust and you have to take the whole baggage. You can decide to leave the whole baggage, but you don't negotiate the baggage.

AMIR: That, to me, is easier to understand, but I think there's something that you said which is more challenging to understand, which is, even if the teacher is wrong—and I take into consideration the possibility that he may be wrong—I still prefer to obey than to rebel.

THOMAS: Only if I trust that overall the context is right. If the whole context is wrong, you have to go. You are alone with that question.

AMIR: In using the term "the overall context," do you mean the teacher's motivation, intention and commitment?

THOMAS: Yes, and perspective.

AMIR: So you're assuming that although they are capable of making mistakes, the ground, which is their perspective and their motivation, is wholesome.

THOMAS: It doesn't have to be perfect. Wholesome is a good word. It's helpful for discrimination.

CHAPTER 8
CHALLENGES AND CRISES

My teacher did not follow the rules, a fact that caused great distress not only to my family and friends but also to other seekers who insisted upon a more conventionally "ethical" path. The rulebook my teacher, his teacher, and even his teacher's teacher adhered to contained only one rule: do whatever is necessary to serve the disciple. It's the rule that absorbs all rules, and has equally been co-opted as an excuse for untold crimes. But ultimately there is little value in playing it safe. Reality isn't safe, and neither are Truth nor God. And there is no way around the fact that you have to play to win.

—MARIANA CAPLAN, *THE GURU QUESTION*

Most wayfarers are taken Home through the simple power of love working within them... but sometimes the ego is too strong to surrender and then the disciple needs to be broken. This is a terrible task for the teacher because the disciple is always dear to the teacher: the link of love holds him or her in your heart. But occasionally instructions are given and this dark work of love begins. It is a subtle process, hardly ever done with any outer show of anger, although sometimes that is necessary. We all have particular weaknesses within us, places where we are vulnerable and afraid. It is here that the teacher begins to pressure the disciple, usually with an energy of cold detachment that can seem heartless. A comment here, a remark there is often all that is needed; sometimes the disciple is simply seemingly ignored for months. There are many ways to break a human being, and when there is great love between teacher and disciple the pain is particularly potent. My teacher called her sheikh her "beloved executioner," so often did he appear hard, cold and distant to her.

You have to be trained to do this work. It is one of the most painful things anyone can be asked to do. And it is done with great love, a love that does not allow anything to get in the way on the road towards Truth. You can also only do this work if it has been done to you. It is the dark side of love, and a work that is much misunderstood. Something within the disciple is destroyed, torn out, crushed. They are broken, made empty.

—LLEWELLYN VAUGHAN-LEE, "WHAT DOES IT MEAN TO BE A TEACHER," STORYMODE.COM

In October 2016, while working on the book, my wife and I stayed for a few days at the ashram of Mooji (Anthony Paul Moo-Young), where he lives with more than 200 of his students, at Monte Sahaja in southern Portugal. The visit gave me an opportunity not only to have a follow-up interview with Mooji, whom I had already interviewed a few months earlier, but also to get a firsthand impression of the relationship between him and some of his closest students.

Mooji is a direct disciple of Sri H.W.L. Poonja (1910-1997), who was an Advaita teacher of Lucknow, India, and a follower of Ramana Maharshi. Like Poonja, a grandfatherly figure who was fondly called "Papaji" by his followers, Mooji is also a loving, warm and generous man. The atmosphere in Mooji's ashram is of love of and service and devotion to the guru. Against this backdrop, it is interesting to consider the stories of challenge and crises, which I heard both from Mooji, when he recounted his meeting with his teacher, and from one of his students.

MOOJI

AMIR: Mooji, before you met your teacher, Poonjaji, did you meet others that had a significant influence on you?

MOOJI: Yes, actually, there was one. As you know, I grew up with a very Christian background in Jamaica, but I would not say I was a practicing Christian, it was just how we grew up. Then in 1987, I met this young man, Michael, who was a devout Christian, but the simplicity of his presence touched me deeply. With him, I had no feeling that I was being manipulated or that anything was expected of me; I just felt like I was talking to a friend. Somehow in his presence certain questions arose that I had never asked before, and his responses satisfied whatever doubts I had.

He lived nearby and we would always meet spontaneously, we never arranged any meeting, and I found it so easy and enjoyable to speak with him. One Sunday evening, at the end of one of these talks, as he was about to leave I asked him, "Michael, when you pray again, will you pray for me?" He responded, "Of course, but why not now?"

I liked that freshness, so I said thank you and we stood up and he put his hand on my forehead and prayed. When he finished, I found myself spontaneously making a prayer—a plea to God for help. After this prayer, a great feeling of lightness filled my being. It was a beautiful, peaceful stillness. Then we hugged and he left, but I felt like I was still being hugged somehow. I felt blissfully happy and light, and I really didn't want to go to sleep for fear that the feeling would go away. So I stayed up as long as I could, but at some point I fell asleep.

I woke up in the morning and was happily surprised that the feeling was still very present. As I lay in bed, I noticed how the sunlight was streaming through a crack in the curtains, and all these little dust particles were floating about in it. It felt like I was looking at the sunlight for the first time. There was a heightened sensitivity in my whole field of perception. It felt wonderful; I felt so fully alive. A deep peace arose in my being—and it has never gone away. Everything felt so miraculous. I felt an urge to share—just to tell someone about how the world was looking through my newfound eyes. I cannot say that my ego died in that experience; it was still there somehow, and occasionally it would just pop up unexpectedly.

Whenever this happened, I would see that things didn't work well when moving from that place. There seemed so much more to learn each and every moment.

So all this started in 1987. Powerful changes began to take place in my life in terms of where I was living, what work would come and the people I would meet along the way. I felt an increasing urge to learn all I could—immediately. One day I went into a famous spiritual bookstore called Watkins in London. Until then I had only ever read two books in my life. There I discovered a book called *The Gospel of Sri Ramakrishna*, which had a strong impact on me. Ramakrishna was from a very different cultural and religious background than me, but his words spoke very clearly and powerfully to my heart, so much so that the fact he was a Hindu and a devotee of the Hindu goddess Kali just bypassed me. Only the truth of what he was speaking was ringing powerfully in my heart and plunged me into this pool of tears and joy. I felt a great love for Ramakrishna.

In those days I didn't have much money, but toward the end of 1993 I did some decorating work for my sister and she gave me what for me was a large sum of money. With that I just bought a ticket and went to India for the first time, with the desire to visit Ramakrishna's place in Kolkata. I actually knew nothing about gurus, except through what was mentioned in Ramakrishna's book. I only had the wish to visit his place and to soak up its atmosphere, a taste of which was already in my heart. I certainly wasn't looking for any teaching or teacher in a conscious way.

AMIR: And on your way there you met Poonjaji?

MOOJI: Yes. Actually I never made it to Kolkata. I was visiting Rishikesh and there I had an unusual meeting with some people who believed they had met me before—though they hadn't. When I arrived to my guesthouse, I found they were checking into the same place, and they invited me to dinner. It was over the meal that they told me about Papaji, of whom they were devotees. That was my first introduction to Papaji, and after that I went to Lucknow to see him.

AMIR: Was your impression of Poonjaji in some way similar to the experience you had with Michael?

MOOJI: Michael spoke about Jesus Christ, with whom I feel great love and affinity. I have a natural attraction to Jesus. But Papaji pointed me to something vast and ineffable within myself. That was very different. It was not an object. It was not a person in that way.

AMIR: Can you speak about Poonjaji's impact on you? Did he have that effect on you immediately?

MOOJI: No, no, it wasn't an immediate love story or anything like that. Actually, when I met Papaji, I was a bit uneasy in his presence, but I knew that the uneasiness was not because there was something strange about him. It was as if something was being revealed in my own nature at the time that was uneasy in his presence. But by that time I was already familiar with such feelings, so it wasn't enough to put me off. So that's why I said it was not love at first sight.

Still, I knew I was in the presence of a very rare being. It was the first time I met someone who carried a presence that was so striking for me. His presence was, unarguably, a very potent phenomenon. It was beyond how I had perceived any human being, and I'm not someone who is very excitable or imaginative in this way. There was just something very clear for me which was embodied in him, like a great light, a very palpable vibration. Actually, in some ways, he reminded me of my mother, who also exuded a similar natural detachment. Papaji was wonderfully, mystically detached, and although he was met with love from so many people, he was not overly affectionate in his expression, not a "huggy" type. This love was coming from a different, deeper, ungraspable place. He carried a stately presence, a beautiful distance, which powerfully draws you in, and yet at the same time fear arises. His presence and the satsangs I experienced with him had a kind of empty quality, which was new for me. Before I met him, my life and being felt full of peace, joy and love, but through Papaji I was experiencing something new—this feeling of spaciousness, an indescribable emptiness. I didn't quite get his teaching, but I was somehow dissolving into this unfathomable empty space that was wiping away any personal history or interest in a personal life.

AMIR: Was there a point in which you recognized him as your teacher?

MOOJI: Yes, but that was after some time. I was really benefiting from being in satsang each day, and I was very touched by this sweet, benevolent power in Papaji's presence, but there was also a part of my mind that was holding him at bay. Eventually, after some months with him, I wrote him a letter. Later that day in satsang he picked up my letter and called me to come up to him, which was in front of maybe 250 people. I was very nervous. He called "Tony," which is my name. Then he said, "That's a girl's name, isn't it?"—he does things like that, you know. I was thinking, "Oh, what is this? Come on!" I was becoming very serious. I went and sat at his feet, and he started reading my letter. Gradually, these unexpected feelings of resistance and judgment began exploding inside because I felt like he was making fun of me. My ego was going, "Whoa, what's this? I've made the effort to write you a sincere letter to introduce myself and you make fun of me!" There was a growing whistling sound inside my head, which became so loud I could no longer hear what Papaji was saying. I could see his lips moving and people laughing, but I really couldn't hear anything. I only picked up at the end that he said, "If you wish to discover the Truth, you must disappear. You must vanish." And that got through, despite my defenses. But all throughout I just felt exposed, shuffled up and humiliated. I didn't like him at all. So in my mind, I was saying: "Yeah, right, that's what I need, because I've been here long enough now and I needed something like this in order to move on."

After this encounter with Papaji, I felt swept aside, as if I was a "nobody." Another questioner came up to replace me at his feet. I really wanted to leave there and then, but I had to wait until the end of satsang. When the end came, I didn't want to talk to anyone. I left hastily for home and started packing my bags feeling, "Okay, fine. It's just what I needed to leave this circus. This is not Lucknow, it's more like 'Bad-Luck-Now.'" I was so enraged, fuming, "This didn't go well at all. I didn't get anything from this encounter."

It was a very hot day, so midway through packing I stopped and went for a walk to the town center. As I was walking along it was like there were sausages frying inside my head, with cold water splashing inside the boiling oil. It felt like hell. I sat under a tree feeling completely shuffled up inside. After a while and without relief I started walking back towards my place, still stuck inside this dark, heavy cloud of anger, frustration and embarrassment—the devil's cocktail.

Suddenly, after maybe twenty steps, everything vanished. All my feelings of anxiety and rage—gone in an instant! Everything—nothing. Nothing of the world I knew, including myself, was present. I could not find any context for my existence, no references to my known world. In one flash—no, not even any flash, there was only this vastness. And yet I was there fully in some clear, formless way. I remember looking at my hands, but it was clear there was no one inside them—strange, yet totally natural. I saw the rickshaws and cars on the road. It appeared as though they were existing inside a parallel dimension, distant and unconnected. Here I was formless, immeasurable, infinite. Out of the vastness an image appeared. It was Papaji. He was infinite too and I suddenly became full of love for him. Later, I realized I hadn't allowed myself to love him before, though I hadn't been fully conscious of it—it was just a survival mechanism for the ego.

In what felt like a timeless instant, there arose inside me this powerful urge to run to Papaji's house and to fall at his feet. I started running like a little schoolboy late for class. I've told this story quite a few times but I am never able to end it conclusively. I don't know what happened; I have no memory of what followed. Each time it all just ends right here in this timeless place.

After this, my attitude and relationship to Papaji changed completely. There was now a lot of space, peace and love for the Master.

AMIR: I'd like to make a big leap forward in time now, and ask you to speak about your relationship with your students.

MOOJI: Let me start by saying that my pointing to people is very simple and direct. It is something that can be immediately experienced rather than something to be believed, or some spiritual philosophy that may take years to understand—it is much more direct than that. My position is the immutable self. This is the core of what guides all my interactions with people who come to me.

Most people come because they have watched satsang YouTube [videos]. Many have read spiritual books and feel they have a good intellectual grasp of things. Now they want only the full and direct experience to end their search. They say, "I come here to experience directly what I understand with my mind. I don't want more intellectual food. I just want to be that. I want to be swallowed up completely." Then I say, "Okay, I think we have a good ground on which we can begin to look together." But I am not looking for any particular relationship with anyone. What is most important is their capacity to grasp what is being pointed to.

People come at varying stages in their own spiritual evolution, and there is patience here for that. There are those whose temperament is more philosophically inclined and to whom the conceptual aspect of self-inquiry is appealing, and there are others whose temperament is more devotional, and I'm deeply comfortable with this also. I don't find any contradiction, for all true paths take the true seeker home. It's quite a spontaneous thing, this intuitive pointing. It may appear to some as being naive or even fickle, but I assure you, it emerges from the very heart of being and has the power to break the grip of psychological identity.

AMIR: How do you work with students who you feel are relatively mature or awake? Do you have any students giving satsang in your name?

MOOJI: It's a good question. At the moment there are six or seven people in different parts of the world sharing what they feel they have grasped through my pointings. I didn't ask them to do this.

They themselves wrote saying that people were asking them questions and they found that the answers were flowing naturally, as if it were I myself responding through them. So I watched some of their exchanges and said, "You may carry on, but beware of any urge to label yourself as a guru or master so that your understanding is not polluted by ego."

After your first awakening experience or profound insight, it's easy to think, "I've done it!" And if you have any arrogance or a cunning mind, your mind quickly believes that its discipleship is over. There are still many seekers who believe themselves to be awake, whereas in fact they are still steeped in delusion. They overlook the signs that expose that personal identity is still alive. Then by the time they realize the mistake, they are already in a role that may feel impossible to get out of without embarrassment or shame. It's so important to take time to mature, and to continue to burn the remnants of the egoic identity, which can linger on and are the last shadows to leave. Therefore, I urge: Continue your inquiry while remaining at the master's feet.

Some students have gone on to become teachers and help others to develop spiritually, but I have not found anyone to guide seekers with the unsparing light and power of self-inquiry in the way that destroys the ego instantly.

The true sharing has no doing or doer behind it, so I don't even know if I will call it sharing. One finds that there is no particular identity to be; identity becomes very superficial and is replaced by a spontaneous, intuitive presence. Whether one speaks with a cat or the baker or someone from satsang, what is shared is always appropriate because it is the spirit that is interacting with varying forms as life. It always functions in perfect timing and takes care of those who love Truth. What I try to protect beings from is any tendency to want to teach at a premature stage in their development, though they may feel within themselves that they are quite ready. This is also the work of the master, to pull the reins on this galloping tendency to rush forward when you should still be sitting in solitude at the master's feet, marinating in presence. Sometimes a seeker or student, having experienced what they feel is a profound insight, then feels that they are somehow qualified to be guiding others. They may even have an urge to set up their own independent group. This is such a huge mistake because it often comes from ego, though it may not be obvious to them in the beginning.

AMIR: Do you ever feel you need to directly challenge a student to go beyond their limitations?

MOOJI: I don't feel that I come to anybody in this way. I feel that a deeper play is taking place. If I'm with someone and I push them beyond *their* perceived limitation, it's because I see space in them to go there. A teacher has to be able to intuitively sense that the perceived limitation is only coming from fear, and guide the student very confidently beyond that perceived limitation. That does happen sometime, when it is clear that it's needed.

AMIR: Does this clarity come to you in a flash, or do you sometimes have to think about the person and consider what's the right thing to do?

MOOJI: I very rarely think about anybody. First of all, I don't think there's anybody. Actually. If I'm being honest, the relationship I have is not from person to person. I don't have this sense. I know clearly that they are consciousness living in a kind of self-portrait as a person. If I believed that I was addressing a person, the evolution or progress would be *minimal*. But because I can address them from the place of presence or consciousness, that's much more effective. It's an altogether different realm and way of working. To me, the person is a deeply limited entity, just a mask.

AMIR: I'm having an interesting experience interviewing you. There's something about the simplicity and directness in which you work with people who come to you, that makes me unsure about my questions. So instead, I'd like to ask you if you feel that there are any issues in your relationship with your students that you don't completely understand.

MOOJI: I am not sure I understand your question. I have no issues as such, and whether there is something I have not really understood in the relationship with students does not concern me. I don't have any set structure or method. My pointing is more of an intuitive, simple process that is rooted in the one single harmony. I'm not requiring anything from students apart from a sense that they are fully open to self-discovery, as much as they have the capacity, or at least the desire and attitude for freedom.

But your question, if there is something I have not really understood in the relationship with students, is actually very relevant at the moment. Because at the moment, some people who had been close students of mine have suddenly just jumped overboard! Sort of, "Sorry, I'm out of here!" So we've had cases like that. Sometimes there are unrecognized or suppressed tendencies and a strong identity survives in the shadows somewhere, and at a certain point it cannot be held anymore and it erupts like this. But I can't say I don't understand that at all, I actually feel that this is a stage in their sadhana.

The initial response is, you know, "How could they have done it?" But very quickly I caught onto that and saw that actually, there is no "they" who have "done" anything, in the true sense. All this is a play of, by and in consciousness. It is crucial that we recognize this and not forget or overlook it. It is consciousness playing the role of a person with dormant, hidden tendencies. Please understand that someone can have an awakening experience and still retain some "person poison." However, I feel this implies a contradiction here, because if those tendencies are alive, they can only be alive in relation to a person, not to presence. And they cannot be alive in that way without being fed, consciously or unconsciously. There must have been a secret feeding of personal identity for it to have prospered and not perished, harboring resistance to true freedom.

AMIR: Are you saying that in some way those people are responsible for the continuation of those tendencies?

MOOJI: You know, I can see it in two ways. One is from the perspective of a person doing something, and the other as a play of consciousness. It is very important to be able to perceive both views. Why is it important to also see from another person's perspective? Because the consciousness in that mode believes in its identity as a person sufficiently to fuel intense desires and want to see them come to fruition. So I have to treat that consciousness in its personal self-belief mode. But I also do not go too far in taking it seriously, because, simultaneously, I know it is just imagination. This protects one from lapsing into states of frustration and disappointment, knowing that it is consciousness appearing in its aspect as *maya* or delusion. Sometimes this play happens, but I see it is not separate from the great harmony. I feel that it is not a question of judging or punishing, but of allowing it to express, perhaps to exhaust its expression, and then perhaps—or perhaps not—realign itself in the real. And I feel that the impact of that experience is useful for everyone, in giving the power to see and grow in wisdom, to learn that nothing is predictable in the realm of phenomenality.

LAKSHMI

LAKSHMI: My name is Lakshmi, I'm thirty-six years old and I met Mooji-ji nine years ago. I was living in Brixton at the time, and someone took me down the road to Mooji-ji's satsang. I had no idea about him, yoga was the sum of my limited knowledge of spiritual teachings. I went to satsang in his house and it was full of people, but somehow a little space opened up right in front of him, so I ended up sitting right at his feet. To be honest, I didn't understand a single word, but I loved him and I couldn't explain that. I kept going, but still I didn't understand anything he was saying. In fact, whenever I tried to ask him any question at the time he would do this [gesture], like flushing it down the toilet. Somehow, this unexplainable love just kept me going to his satsangs. Then I moved to Monte Sahaja, just where it started, forty-five years ago, and I'm now one of Guru-ji's personal assistants and I also help with the development of Sahaja in different areas.

AMIR: Since not everybody who met Mooji and had a powerful experience or connection with him chose to move and live close to him, like you did, I'm interested to know why you made that choice.

LAKSHMI: For me, it wasn't really a choice. Thankfully, life just brought me here, and the more I recognize who Guru-ji is, the less I can see any other avenue of life that would compare to living with him. The closer I watch him, the more he starts to come inside me and I start to see through his eyes and love with his heart. It's like a magnet pulling you, and it almost feels like there isn't really a choice. If your heart says yes to what he's pointing to, then it just flows in that direction and your life goes with it.

AMIR: What do you mean by "he starts to come inside me"? Can you give me some examples?

LAKSHMI: Guru-ji is always proving to me, on a practical level and very subtly, that he's listening from inside of me. One time I was upset about something and wanted to tell him, but it was very early in the morning. Still, I was consumed by this thing so I went and I sat outside his house. Of course I didn't want to wake him up, but I had to tell him. I was there for maybe five minutes when my phone rang, and it was Guru-ji, and he said, "I just felt to call you." Then he let me in and I could share this thing with him. He often does things like that. One time I was preparing his food, and I had this thought, "I hope I don't burn this!" and then I heard him from across the room: "Lakshmi, don't burn that!" He makes these small gestures to let me know, to confirm that he's listening from inside. Another time I was thinking about some darker aspects of the mind that I don't want Guru-ji to see, and just as I thought that, he said out loud: "Don't worry about those things, they don't mean anything to me." So it's an inner thing, he's waking up here, speaking from here, listening to me from here. [She points to herself.] The whole experience is very much here. Even though I love to be in his physical presence, the fundamental experience is happening here, inside. It's like water pouring, pouring like this, if that makes sense. [She giggles.] Sorry, I'm feeling a lot of joy.

AMIR: Would you say that each of us has the potential to be awake and enlightened as Mooji is?

LAKSHMI: I guess it must be possible! This whole ashram is being built up just for this purpose. Of course, it must lead to us recognizing our true nature, and I see we are moving in this direction. If I look to who we are now, five years on from the beginning of Sahaja, the deepening of the space, the emptiness that people move in, there is a maturing in this. Where it ends, I don't know, but it must be possible.

AMIR: Since you had such a strong connection with Mooji right from when you met him, in that sense nothing changed, right? So when you speak of "moving," what is this movement?

LAKSHMI: Um, I can't say that is true. I only know Guru-ji as much as my capacity allows, and it deepens, deepens and deepens. Now I have enough experience to know that even when I know him, I still don't know him. You can't reach the bottom of who he is. When I first met him, I could not understand what he was saying, I had no idea what he was talking about, but love held me to him and I remember that moment when there was nothing, just nothing. Has that changed? No, but there are definitely different subtleties of understanding, and they're incomparable. I've been moving on with Guru-ji and there is something that's deepening and becoming subtler, especially in my inquiry—much more than when I first met him, or even last year, or even in my last India retreat experience. Something is becoming more and more subtle. Does that make sense?

AMIR: Yes, it does. And is this process always and only natural and spontaneous, or do you sometimes have to make some effort? Is it sometimes challenging, confronting, difficult?

LAKSHMI: Oh, definitely! Sometimes the identity needs to be chopped. You might not even know that you're invested in some corner of identity, because you're devotional also in this aspect. And yet, Guru-ji can see that there is some identity hidden there, and he would chop it. Of course, these moments are not easy. It feels like you have had an operation, something has to rearrange itself in you. It can be very painful. But what's left is just less of you.

If we talk about surrender and devotion, I'm moving in this way, taking instructions from Guru-ji, and with all my heart and devotion following them, but what I perhaps don't realize is that there is an identity still attached to that, and I'm interpreting myself through some kind of conditioning, following the instructions through an identity, which is wrapped in my love and my devotion. So when it's revealed that you're operating from mind and not from heart, it's painful but also very revealing.

AMIR: Did you ever want to run away?

LAKSHMI: Okay—once. Actually, this is what I'm talking about. I think everyone at a certain point in their relationship with Guru-ji comes to a point when an aspect of identity comes up, and it's almost like it comes with power. You're told that you should follow your experience. Then some experience comes up and your mind is convinced that this is true. It's in those moments that the Sangha and Guru-ji really serve you, if you can hear them.

I had an experience when this came up, and Guru-ji was challenging me in this aspect, which for me felt very real at the time. I trust him fully, and this doesn't falter, and yet the experience of the identity was so strong that for a moment I had to walk away. I just had to walk away. But because I knew that Guru-ji wasn't with it, I knew I couldn't trust it, even if the experience was so real. I did go with it, but it disintegrated within a short time, a day.

It really revealed a lot. After all the years, the mind was still expressing itself—wanting to be someone through devotion, through service. Identity was reinventing itself in subtle ways. By grace, Guru-ji saw it and didn't allow it to continue. So, yes, I ran away—for a day—and then came back very grateful, because it was so revealing to see these things. Now I see they are still playing out, but because Guru-ji exposed them, it's now very easy to see when they come, so they don't have as much life.

AMIR: It sounds like you're learning about the human condition, about how the desire to become somebody keeps operating in us even in the face of so much love and light.

LAKSHMI: I think we're learning that there is another way to move, that is independent of the mind's function. Learning about the mind is a byproduct, but that's happening while something else is deepening. Not so much attention is put on human nature and the mind. What's happening here is more learning to be empty and being comfortable with that.

In the literature of the Tibetan and Zen traditions, as well as of other mystical traditions, some of the most well-known accounts of the teacher-student relationship stress the teacher's wildness, unpredictability and use of "shock therapy" techniques aimed at inducing a psychological-spiritual crisis. The behavior of those teachers appears, from a conventional perspective, as harsh, abusive and even sadistic, but within those traditions, it is recognized as necessary to release the disciple from the grip of his ego and allow for enlightenment or liberation to occur.

Some nontraditional modern-day spiritual teachers have also taken crisis induction as part of their job description. This was definitely the case with my former teacher, Andrew Cohen, during my time with him. Priding himself on being a ruthlessly uncompromising teacher, he pushed many of his students into the proverbial corner—unfortunately inducing, in most cases, a breakdown rather than a breakthrough, and leaving people spiritually and emotionally shattered. Still, many of his students—myself included—benefited enormously from this teaching tactic.

One of the several crises I went through took place in Sydney, Australia, in 2001. After being Andrew's student for over a dozen years, it was clear to him and to my friends in our community that one of the strongholds of my ego-personality was my belief in my sincere and profound commitment to a life of Truth and liberation, and that this self-image was preventing me from seeing the fact that my persona included also the very opposite impulses and motives. Whenever I had to face indications that this was the case, I would internally split—taking the position of a fundamentally and profoundly "good" person seeing a blemish in themselves that they immediately and unhesitatingly want to renounce. Andrew's and my friends' attempts to show me that, like every human being, I was a complex whole that included different and contradictory impulses and motives, only caused me to become more entrenched in the split position, to everybody's dismay.

Over the years I had spent with Andrew, this tendency (or choice) to split in the face of reflection from my friends was the root cause of several crises I went through. Ultimately, it led Andrew to send me to a center our organization had in Sydney, Australia, which for a short period of time served as our community's "penal colony" (ironically, just as Australia once had for Great Britain), hosting several of Andrew's long-term students on whom he wanted to put extra pressure.

I arrived in Sydney with only $200 in my pocket and without any idea when and how I would start making money again, a fact that contributed to my general misery. The other students of Andrew who were at the center, some of whom had been my close friends since our early days in the community, started without delay to pressurize me to face what I had been unwilling to face up to that point—that I was a mixed bag, just like every other human being. Under their pressure, as well as the pressure of my fear of being kicked out and finding myself on the street without any money, I only dug in deeper. A few months later I had more money (fortunately I was offered a translation project that refilled my wallet), but psychologically I was finding the situation I was in more and more unbearable.

Then one day, sitting on the beach, I decided to leave Andrew and the community, and move back to Israel. I vividly remember the physical sensation I had when I made that decision—every cell in my body released the tension that had been stored in it for months and years, and I felt as though I stepped under a waterfall of pure, cold water that was washing away all my anxiety and fear. It was total relief. I started walking back to the center, thinking of how I was going to tell my friends there about my decision, of what I was going to write Andrew, of letting my parents know I was moving back to Israel, when something totally unexpected happened. I lowered my head to pass under a tree branch that was over the sidewalk, and when I straightened up again I suddenly saw the whole picture and realized what Andrew and my friends had been trying to tell me for ages: that I had created the division in myself and continuously fed the big drama of the "good" part in me fighting the "bad" part, that it was all untrue, and that everybody could see that except me, because I hadn't wanted to give up my self-image. I knew at that moment that I was seeing everything I needed to see in order to be free of the inner struggle and to release everybody around me from it as well.

So significant was that revelation, that I felt it had changed me for good. I decided not to tell my friends about what had happened, but to let myself and them find out about the impact of such an event. It was only a week later when, in a meeting we had at the center, my friends asked me: "Amir, what happened to you about a week ago? You seem completely different—relaxed, real, warm, a joy to be around—what happened?" Only then did I tell them about the event on the beach and the tree branch.

A few months later I was back with the community in the U.S. Much more importantly, though, was the insight I had gained into the mechanics of splitting within myself, which has since enabled me to better understand myself and many others with a similar tendency.

Is it necessary to be confronted and challenged by a radical teacher in order to go through psycho-spiritual crises and gain insight into the depth of our conditioned, fearful responses to the possibility of freedom, authenticity and wholeness? It seems to me that the crisis Mooji underwent while with Poonjaji, and the crisis Lakshmi underwent while with Mooji, were not intentionally evoked by the teachers. Can we say that they were induced (albeit unconsciously) by the students? Were they a spontaneous result of the psychologically- and spiritually-charged dynamics of the teacher-student relationship?

If, indeed, psycho-spiritual crises tend to occur spontaneously as part of the teacher-student relationship, and maybe even as part of the spiritual quest, life and practice, this has significant implications for both those teachers who regard crisis induction part of their job description, and those who blame teachers for ruthlessly and irresponsibly inducing crises in their students.

CHAPTER 9
MUTUALITY AND HIERARCHY

One of the great principles of Hasidism is that the zaddik [righteous] and the people are dependent on one another... Here we come to the very foundation of Hasidism, on which the life between those who quicken, and those who are quickened, is built up. The quintessence of this life is the relationship between the zaddik and his disciples, which unfolds the interaction between the quickener and the quickened in complete clarity. The teacher helps his disciples find themselves and in hours of desolation the disciples help their teacher find himself again. The teacher kindles the souls of his disciples and they surround him and light his life with the flame he has kindled. The disciple asks, and in his manner of asking unconsciously evokes a reply, which his teacher's spirit would not have produced without the stimulus of the question.

—**MARTIN BUBER**, *ON INTERSUBJECTIVITY AND CULTURAL CREATIVITY*

Mutual surrender is a process in which teacher and student surrender to each other, each in his or her own way and to the extent of his or her own capacity, ever deepening that surrender until the distinction between teacher and student disappears fully in essence, remaining only in form.

—**MARIANA CAPLAN**, *THE GURU QUESTION*

SANIEL BONDER

I conducted four consecutive interviews with Saniel Bonder, totaling more than six hours. In the following excerpt, we explored the question of mutuality and hierarchy in his experiences as a student of Adi Da and as a founding teacher and a colleague in the Waking Down in Mutuality network:

AMIR: Let's begin with you as a student. Did you have teachers before you met Adi Da?

SANIEL: Yes, I did. He was certainly my main in-life human-to-human teaching relationship far and away, and I spent almost twenty years with him, but there had been several teachers before him. To properly acknowledge my sources, I have to say my relationship with my father was in many ways a teacher-student relationship, and in later years it dawned on me that there was quite a transmission I received from him, although he was not a spiritually self-aware person.

Then, in my high school years, I went to a small private school in a very small village in the state of Tennessee, and the headmaster there and a couple of the teachers were also very formative influences on me, at a deeper level than merely the content of the courses they taught.

Then what occurred in my life as spiritual student was that I had the beginning of a religious and spiritual awakening when I was twenty, and fairly quickly my initial sources were American transcendentalists, mainly Walt Whitman from the nineteenth century and Allen Ginsberg and Ken Kesey of *The Electric Kool-Aid Acid Test* fame of the twentieth century. Martin Buber was also a crucial influence in terms of what later became the mutuality side of my work, the emphasis on relationships, as was Thomas Merton. Another important influence, as I began to move toward the East, was Paramahansa Yogananda's book, *Autobiography of a Yogi*. After reading it, I became principally attracted to the Hindu style of the Guru-disciple relationship.

But the real action for me in terms of what became my prominent, primary lineage was finding Ramana Maharshi's teaching. Even though he was physically no longer with us, his transmission was quite activating for me and I became a devotee of Ramana for about a year and a half. Toward the end of that time it was dawning on me that I needed a human master, but I felt I had to find someone who also knew about the heart as Ramana spoke of it, as the Divine essence and nature of all and everything. That's what then led me to Adi Da's work, back when he was Bubba Free John, and I spent nineteen-plus years with him.

AMIR: If you go back to when you were looking for a teacher, what was it that you were looking for? Why did you feel you needed to find more after reading a lot and meeting a lot of teachers through reading? Why did you feel it was necessary to be with a living teacher?

SANIEL: Once I came in contact with the more mystical yoga tradition, it made sense to me that the ideal way to go about this was under the direct tutelage of someone who can transmit the nature of that realization to you. Actually, the reason I regard myself as a disciple of Ramana Maharshi was because I was receiving his transmission continuously. Later, it dawned on me that Ramana was kind of paragon of ancient India, and here I was in the early 1970s in America, with innumerable questions about sexuality, career, diet, family, how to live a human life, etc. That was when I came upon Adi Da's work, and on the first page of Adi Da's autobiography, *The Knee of Listening*, he spoke of the Heart and said, "I am That." That immediately and completely captivated me. and I got that book and *The Method of the Siddhas*, his second book, at the same time, read them in a weekend, and just knew that he was the one for me.

AMIR: Did you meet him personally soon after?

SANIEL: Yes, I did. Pretty much immediately after reading his books, in early October 1973, I wrote to the then-still-young community in California that I felt he was my guru and applied to become a student, or whatever it was called in that context. A few months later, the person who was my assisting representative in California challenged me to come out immediately to join the community, because I was asking questions about what vitamins I should take while they had begun this rather uproarious, Tantric adventure. Terry Patten and I later were the editors of a book about it, called *Garbage and the Goddess*. The guy who interviewed me basically felt I was a hopeless case unless I came out there. That created some difficulty with my family, because I left my teaching job in New Orleans pretty much on the spot, breaking my contract, but at that time, and me being me, my priority was to get out there at all cost. When I arrived there, I immediately walked into a party and was given a beer and a cigarette, and as I walked through the door, I said, "Okay, now I understand why the question about which kind of vitamin E I should use might not be so relevant."

AMIR: Was Adi Da there?

SANIEL: Yes, he was in the room and eventually invited me to come up and offer my gifts, so I gave him all the gifts I could, but he kept holding out his hand for more. So I jumped on his lap, gave him a hug, and that was the beginning of the primary teaching relationship of my life.

AMIR: From all I heard and read, this relationship took hierarchy to the extreme. How did you cope with that?

SANIEL: It's true that later on he gravitated into what became one of the most top-down relationships in spiritual history, but in the early years of his work he proposed to be teaching more as a friend than as a guru. That's why he took that old-time Southern nickname Bubba, which his father had called him, and called himself Bubba Free John. But even then he was always reserving a special place for himself, even when it was all about being brotherly and friendly and mixing it up with people informally, so as to make room for our growth and help us through our purification on various levels.

He did make the point, though, that the means to the goal of radical understanding, which was his phrase for the realization of unity, was satsang with the guru. But in those early years he had not yet taken to radically, definitively and conclusively proclaiming that he was himself the realizer and the embodiment of the conscious principle or the core of the Self-nature for his students or devotees. He became more absolutist about all that as time went on, and ultimately proposed to be the one and only Guru of all time, past, present and future. You know, it was, "I am not only the guru but the ultimate guru, and existentially you are not in any way, shape or form my true equal." We could go into how he got there and what persuaded him, because it wasn't merely egoic narcissism. You can't reduce it to just that, as you well know, having studied with a powerful teacher.

Anyway, I know it sounds absurd, and for me it was increasingly challenging, but there were a lot of intelligent people who took him very seriously, because we saw the depth and complexity in the man. I also loved the devotional relationship in many ways, and there was a great deal of ecstatic enjoyment that took place with him, both in personal contact and living as a devotee.

AMIR: So when and why did you part ways with him?

SANIEL: I left Adi Da in 1992 under challenging circumstances. I physically separated from the community, and then I had to go through a kind of psycho-spiritual separation that took quite a bit longer. What led to that is a complex story. Over the years, Adi Da became increasingly convinced that those of us who were longer-time devotees were failed cases. He ceased to have very much hope that we could awaken in this lifetime. And for me, I had certainly thrown myself joyfully into the devotional relationship that he asked for, but to me it was always the means to the end of my own awakening. And as the years went on and he increasingly regarded me among those who didn't have what it took to awaken in his context, I became increasingly sobered by what I felt was in effect my guru telling me, "Good luck, just practice, because you're not going to get there in this lifetime." I had not come in order to just be an eternal devotee, which is where he took his work, it was what he wanted us to choose and aspire to.

At a deeper level, a crisis emerged in 1991, which was a few years before he gave himself the name Adi Da Samraj, which means "king of everything." I began to be sobered by the fact that I had lost touch with some of my previous values that I had gotten from my earlier teachers—including my parents and teachers when I was a boy or a teenager—related to personal integrity. At some point it became evident that I was willing to be a kind of bureaucratic liar playing political in order to acquire the favor of the guru. This became unacceptable to me. I didn't know at that time that you don't leave Adi Da's work with a gold watch and a pat on the back for your twenty years of service. It was more "You leave here and it will take you many lifetimes of hellish suffering until you come back," because of breaking the master-disciple or guru-devotee connection, that bond.

AMIR: And then you went quite to the other extreme and founded Waking Down in Mutuality, a teaching structure and a spiritual community that's decidedly egalitarian, with as little hierarchy as possible.

SANIEL: What happened was that a few months after I came out of that, I went through a spiritual awakening, which I relate to as "my second birth." And I realized that I never did fit there in Adi Da's work, I never had. As I looked back on my history there, I could see that I always had a more democratic kind of orientation, which sometimes got me into trouble. So I resolved to see how much we can democratize awakening, what we can do if we make mutuality a governing principle. But what I meant by that was not to eliminate all forms of hierarchy. For me, it was never about becoming purely egalitarian. But it was about being participant-centered, rather than guru-centered, and about being democratic and based on mutuality. I think the word "democratic" makes room for hierarchical elements.

AMIR: Would you be willing to tell me about the difficulties you had in maintaining such a structure? I know that quite recently the organization went through some kind of a crisis related to the issue of mutuality versus hierarchy. We know a lot about the difficulties inherent in a hierarchical structure, but could you shed some light on what the difficulties are in a democratic structure of a spiritual community?

SANIEL: Yes, we have recently gone through such a crisis. Thankfully, we've managed it so it was a step of evolutionary differentiation. What used to be the Waking Down Teachers Association renamed itself and is now called Trillium Awakening. Thankfully, everybody worked hard to keep it from being cataclysmic at the level of destroying the work, and the work is very much going on and we're all trying to move forward.

You see, I never was under the impression that I was just looking for peer egalitarianism with people. For one thing, I was always aware that I was bringing something to the situation that others weren't. This, I think, became a part of the issue, especially with some of the leading, more senior teachers. Then there were different aspects of what I was bringing in that I wound up suppressing, in order to make the democratization possible. Those, then, were no longer suppressible.

AMIR: What were they?

SANIEL: From very early on, I got that there were certain potentials of the teacher-student relationship connection that had been very front and center for me, both with Ramana Maharshi and with Adi Da. There was a very profound devotional potential for me, explicit in both of their teachings, although it became more and more prominent with Adi Da. The nature of that connection is not egalitarian, and it's not simply to help someone get to another state. It actually is a very profound relationship. When the mystery dimension of it is given room to breathe, it becomes a form of mutual recognition and love and commitment that is so mysterious.

Now, part of what I saw happening in our work as it evolved was that in order to make room for democratization to take place, in the era when so many people had been wounded by the abuses of hierarchical structures, I had to bite my tongue or hold back those qualities of my natural expression and orientations. Then certain students came to me with a recognition that: "There is something about this connection I feel with you that isn't getting addressed in the work in general, or even by you very much. It's not just about how you can help me get more awake. There is a relationship here that has its own value that I really want to explore." And I knew it couldn't be any other way, given the lineage that I came out of, as well as my own nature. Because, for me, devotion is a natural expression of my being; and in the situation we created, there wasn't really room for that to be naturally and fully expressed.

AMIR: The question is, though, how you interpret the devotion to the master. Is it devotion to his or her personality and you're taking it all, hook, line and sinker, or are you making distinctions between the personality and what comes through that personality?

SANIEL: Some of the liabilities in what I call "the mythic romance of the Absolute Person," which Adi Da cultivated, is that you are moved to proclaim at some point that you are beyond karma: "Everything and anything I do is nothing but the divine." Some people don't mind saying that, and the way they hold structures of accountability with their disciples loads up all of the shadow of both parties on the student, until the situation becomes completely unworkable.

I'll tell you a story about Adi Da that exemplifies it, that was something I experienced firsthand as an editor, working closely with him. Up until the big transition he went through in 1986, he was always saying, "When you're editing my talks, you have to discern what kind of reference I'm making. If I'm talking about the 'me' that is essentially Franklin Jones the man, then that *me* needs to be lower case. But if I'm talking about the ultimate Heart-nature then it should be capitalized, the divine *Me*." Later, after 1986, everything became capitalized.

As for myself—I'm using myself as an example—I know myself well as a divinely realized adept, I know what spiritual transmission is and what it can do, and I'm taking greater and greater responsibility for it. I'm also—and there isn't a dividing line in there somewhere, it's all one piece—a guy with issues and wounds. You don't get through life without damage, so there's no reason to pretend. Actually, I don't think Adi Da was pretending. I feel he had a major blind spot. He never did any formal psychological work in relationship with a competent therapist or analyst, and it didn't occur to him to seriously do an investigation along such lines. He just presumed himself to be completely superior to it, not because psychological self-understanding didn't matter, but because he assumed only he could conduct it with sufficient wisdom for and in himself.

AMIR: I'd like to look with you at two goals that a teacher has in their work with the student: One is to facilitate the process of individuation and support the student in their coming to being an independent, discriminating free person, and the other is to provide the student with the conditions for submission and surrender to that which is beyond their opinions and personal preferences. And these two goals seem to contradict each other. You spent nearly twenty years in a model that very much gave the student the experience of submission and surrender, and can testify to the virtues and disadvantages of that model, and then you created a model that went the opposite way, and have been trying that for the last twenty years, so you can probably testify to the virtues and disadvantages of that model as well.

SANIEL: We're talking about the spiritual teacher-student relationship, referring to teachers who surrendered into a condition in which they can't but acknowledge their identification with the great unity, and to a student who intuitively feels that's what they want. In such a situation we're operating from the very roots of the soul. It's utterly, profoundly intimate and extremely vulnerable for the student; and those of us who presume to take responsibility for teaching are saddled with an enormously daunting task, of trying to give the student every possible opportunity and access to that realized identification.

For me, if I view the first twenty-two to twenty-three years of my work as, hopefully, a first great phase, if I was erring in that phase it was too much, yes, in the direction of "Let's make equality our priority here." It's so interesting to be having this conversation with you, because literally right now I'm at a stage in my thinking where I'm going in the direction of telling people, at least at times and under certain conditions, "This is what you should do and it's not negotiable."

I should add here: It's not that we didn't make any requirements of people whatsoever, like saying to people that they should read this or that book before they can enter into this or that program. But what I'm talking about here is more in the realm of getting people to do things that they wouldn't ordinarily choose to do. As one writer on personal development put it, getting people to move beyond the entrepreneurial kind of approach, which is doing what comes naturally to one as one sees fit, into what he calls the more purposeful approach, of "You've got to be willing to do what comes unnaturally." In this domain, as in many others, that's best served by having someone who has already traversed the territory and is likely to be more skilled than you are at choosing that "unnatural path."

AMIR: How do you do that without allowing the student to abdicate responsibility?

SANIEL: That's where the teacher-student relationship becomes a day-to-day, hour-to-hour, moment-to-moment process. Both parties are aware of both kinds of virtue needing to be cultivated and are figuring out together, through dialogue, which needs emphasis at any given moment. I'm contemplating saying to people, "If you're willing, I think what we need to do in order to get to the next phase of our project, and it's for the sake of something we're cultivating together, is that we need for me to tell you this is what you need to do, and you need to give it a whirl even though it may feel very unnatural to you." In such a moment, the person in the student position essentially has to agree to at least temporarily abdicate exclusively personal responsibility, or the autonomy to make their own choices, and to submit. We would then want to maintain communication, so we don't get into the dangers of taking either orientation to the extreme, which guarantees a shadow distortion.

AMIR: What you're suggesting is not that there would be a period of time in which the student submits wholesale, but an ongoing negotiation of that position from one situation to another.

SANIEL: In general, yes, even if, for instance, the two agree that the student is going to undergo a certain kind of discipline for a period of time, or until such and such changes, or evidence would indicate that that stage is over and we need to move to something new. You see, I think that for those of us who serve as teachers, if we are hidden behind a shield of projected infallibility, always knowing best, then we're not actually meeting the student. It's a challenging business.

PETER BAMPTON

My friendship with Peter Bampton began when he joined Andrew Cohen's community a couple of years after I did. It was briefly interrupted when Pete left the community after thirteen years, and renewed when I eventually left the community a few years later. Since then, we've had many long conversations, during which I learned how he and his wife, Cynthia, bought an abandoned farm in central Portugal, which gradually became the center of a growing spiritual-ecological community, and that he and Cynthia were experimenting with their roles within that community. I was particularly interested to find out how, after all those years of being around an authoritative guru-type teacher like Andrew, Pete dealt with the question of hierarchy in his own community.

AMIR: This interview should be especially interesting because I know you as a student of Andrew Cohen, and now I'm getting to know you as a teacher. Let's start with you as a student: What led to your meeting with Andrew, and how did you become his student?

PETER: Before I met Andrew I had gotten to a point in my life where spiritual liberation, enlightenment, whatever that mystery was, was the most important thing to me. I had almost become a Buddhist monk a year before in Amaravati, a Theravada Buddhist monastery in England under the guidance of Ajahn Sumedho, but I went through a crisis at the monastery. It had to do with the fact that, while I had no doubt about the clarity and intent of the Buddha Dharma, the teaching, I began to have doubts about what I was seeing in terms of how it was lived in the monastery. One thing led to another and one day it became very clear to me that, "Oh my God, this isn't it, and I'm not going to become a monk." This was a shattering realization at the time, because I had already left everything behind, I had been travelling for years and no longer had any roots or friends to speak of in the U.K. So I was really alone, and I was in this crisis of what to do next.

It was during that period that I read *I Am That* by Sri Nisargadatta at the monastery, and its pure, radical transmission of freedom here and now had a huge impact on me. That book awakened me to the radical immediacy of enlightenment and it opened up for me the whole question of a teacher. I became very interested in finding a master, but of course Nisargadatta was gone, Krishnamurti was gone, and one night I prayed for what felt like the first time in my life although I had been raised as a Catholic. I remember being in my room in a state of desperate longing, and I was reading a book, *Daughter of Fire* by Irina Tweedie. I was reading what the guru said, which was about that Indian saying that "when the student is ripe the guru will appear," and I just went into a spontaneous prayer that overwhelmed me.

The next day I went into the library of the monastery and started looking in the miscellaneous section, which is mostly tarot cards and vegetarian cooking, and I found Andrew's book *My Master Is My Self*. I took this book back to my room and devoured it. I had a radical awakening reading that book and I knew that this was it, I'd found my teacher and my teacher had found me. It was absolutely doubtless. It was like grace beyond anything I could have imagined. Luckily, there was an address in the book, and I remember writing him a letter and putting it in the mailbox, suddenly thinking, "Am I completely crazy? What is going on here?" Then I just let it go.

AMIR: How do you see the connection between your prayer and coming upon Andrew's book and responding so dramatically to it?

PETER: If I look back on what happened then there was a mysterious synchronicity about it. My longing for liberation was so one-pointed and I was so genuinely and sincerely desperate after realizing that I was not going to be ordained as a monk, so it was like I called it forth. It was both my intention and a complete readiness and willingness to surrender, at least at that time when I discovered that book. I've always said that when I read the book *My Master Is My Self*, that's when I met my teacher, but of course really I just "met" my own true self. This occurred before I met Andrew in physical form, so that recognition completely transcended any relationship and yet his descriptions of his own awakening catalyzed my own at the time.

I remember after I had read the book going for a walk in an expanded, ecstatically shattered state and I had a direct realization that I had never existed. I saw that I had never been separate and that the apparent trajectory of my personal story had never actually occurred. It was the death of a separate "me." I remember looking up to the sky and my conscious experience of "I" included everything, the sky was my self and everything was my self. And in this nondual recognition there was also the presence of a vast cosmic intelligence that exerted a demand, the sense that "Not my will but Thy Will be Done." It was absolutely terrifying and profoundly liberating at the same time, I'll never forget it.

So all that happened to me before I met him physically, and in terms of how that relationship took root in my soul, if you like, it was prior to my relationship with him on the personal time-bound level. And when I met Andrew in the flesh, four-five months later, interestingly—and I'll never forget this—when he walked into the room I had a very tacit recognition that we had already met. So it was very profound and mysterious right from the beginning. I soon afterward surrendered to him as my teacher and moved into his community in Marin County.

AMIR: And what role did the relationship with Andrew play in your life from that point on?

PETER: Looking back, I can see that it was the teaching that was more primary for me than my personal relationship with Andrew as a teacher. I think that was because I intuitively knew that the awakening that had happened to me transcended our relationship and it was also probably because at the time I met him he was emphasizing an impersonality both in his teachings and in our relationships with him. So while he was definitely in the "guru" position for me, this never resulted in a kind of "guru devotion" for his person. So it was primarily the clarity of his teaching that lit me up then. I still consider some aspects of his teachings and especially the work we engaged in that was focused on the higher potentials of collective awakening to be groundbreaking contributions in the Western enlightenment Dharma. He was able to communicate certain aspects of what awakening is all about in a precise and uncompromising way that was quite extraordinary, but there were other aspects of himself and his teaching that were undeveloped that ultimately led to all kinds of problems.

But with all that said, the direct relationship with him was at the core of the whole adventure and it was heaven and hell. He pushed me very hard. I'll never forget him saying in front of everybody, after I'd been a student for two or three years: "Do you see how much potential this guy has, how much understanding, how much depth? But do you also see how selfish he is?" After that, the next ten years were all about that dichotomy. I went through extraordinary challenges with Andrew, including running away and coming back a few times. Looking back, I see plenty of ways in which he was sometimes needlessly harsh and lacking empathy, but in terms of me and my story, I have no regrets whatsoever, and I'll always be grateful that I did choose the teacher who was radical and willing to push me to the wall.

I had the strength of spirit and intention to come through those crises, and I think it was because, what else was I going to do? One time when the pressure was overwhelming, I left and ended up in the Buddhist monastery again and put myself on retreat there. That was kind of symbolic, because there I was, where I'd been ten years before, and I saw all the ways in which my ego was trying to convince me that somehow I could go backwards in time. It was a big crisis for me, where I faced into the enormity of my ego-resistance, my selfishness and arrogance. Through that very intense confrontation, with all the forces of resistance and selfishness in myself, something broke open and shifted at the core of my being, and from then on, I experienced a deepening continuum of surrender that has unfolded to this day. In simple terms, it was a letting go of my "personal enlightenment project" and a shift into becoming a giver, letting go of control and realizing that this life and whatever I understood spiritually was never for me in the first place. I don't think I would have never gotten anywhere near that depth of surrender without being under the tutelage of a radical teacher, despite all his imperfections.

AMIR: Did your relationship develop or deepen over your time with him?

PETER: That is an interesting question, because in retrospect I see that the relationship did not really develop or deepen, and that was largely why I ended up leaving Andrew. I remained his student for around two years after the crisis I just described, and I was willing and ready to give myself both to him and to the organization, EnlightenNext, in a way I never had until that point. Although Andrew hinted at giving me new opportunities to participate in a creative way, they never materialized, and also my relationship with him did not deepen that much either. Over time, I began to feel creatively suppressed. I felt that my awakening was not going to unfold organically within the structures of the organization and the community, and the hierarchical relationship with Andrew, so these things along with a number of other factors led me to eventually take the decision to leave.

AMIR: Could you tell me a bit about what happened when you left Andrew?

PETER: Well, that is also quite mysterious, because my leaving him as a student catalyzed the beginning of a fuller expression of the awakening process I had undergone as his student. Leaving Andrew as my teacher, and the community of spiritual brothers and sisters that had been my home for thirteen years, was the hardest decision I ever made in my life. Yet through the insecurity and trauma of being essentially alone again, without any clear direction ahead, there was a deep stillness and intuitive trust that this was the next and necessary step. I resolved to be as true as I could to my deepest understanding, and through that, I relaxed into an organic life-flow that took me into a further adventure of awakening.

Fast-forward: I ended up on the island of Ibiza, Spain, and got together with my now-wife Cynthia, who was also a former student of Andrew Cohen who had recently left [him], and we ended up taking almost two years of retreat, letting go of everything, making space for whatever wanted to emerge next. I consciously let go of all ideas about what I should be or what should occur. For whatever reason, I had enough trust in my own motivation to let myself go very deeply.

Then a vision to create a project that would be a convergence of all of our learning and passions began to emerge. We came to Portugal and bought an abandoned farm, and here we are, eight years later, with a thriving project that now includes four resident communities and the committed involvement of around sixty people dedicated to integral spiritual awakening. I could have never imagined that this would all unfold. All through that time, as the project was developing, I didn't have the notion of being a teacher, all I wanted to do was to give. I felt I've got so much to give, and I knew that was why I was here.

AMIR: Was there a point in which you became a teacher, or realized you were a teacher?

PETER: A significant point was the time I gave a presentation on "Conscious Evolution" at the Boom Festival, which was about four years after we arrived in Portugal. There were about fifty people who had come, and I remember something just came roaring out of me when I was speaking. My experience was that all the depth and power of what I learned in that progressive spiritual experiment was there and streaming through me. I'll never forget walking back to the car after that, thinking, "Oh my God, what just happened there?" I was overwhelmed. I was bearing witness to something that was my deepest Self, capital S, and that was obviously far greater than me in any small sense, and I felt an incredible demand coming from my own true self to surrender. And that occurred consciously at a deep level then. From then on, I knew I had a vocation to teach that had nothing to do with me choosing to be a teacher.

After that I began to teach in earnest. And interestingly, it was not only because I began to take the initiative, people also started asking me to teach. I was traveling a lot, I gave talks and taught meditation retreats and put a whole course together, and that's mainly what I was doing, teaching mostly in Lisbon and Porto. I was doubtless about it, totally behind it. It all felt completely effortless and people were coming and being deeply impacted, many of them are long-term co-creators of the Awakened Life Project and members of our Awakened Sangha. So, all of that happened and it continues. I knew from the impact that I was having on people that what I was doing was real and authentic, and so I have just allowed it to unfold organically. I think part of why our project has grown and developed, is that Cynthia and I are upholding an absolute principle of nonduality with a certain authority, while at the same time not suggesting in any way notions of human perfection, whatever that would mean. The foundation of the Awakened Life Project is the nondual ground of non-separation and the radical immediacy of freedom here and now, even if that doesn't seem to be how things are at any given moment.

AMIR: Where does that authority that you mentioned come from, in your experience?

PETER: Much of my authority comes from my recognition, over time, that while I still had the capacity to act out of self-serving ego-based motives, my egoic "I" was no longer the primary driver of this human vehicle. Once I had left my teacher, and what revealed itself to be a constricting communal environment, my own awakening flowered and reconfigured my orientation to life in such a way that I knew the egoic motive to "be somebody" and have a narcissistic orientation to spiritual awakening had been displaced, and that was something that I could trust in terms of my own motivation.

The other important aspect is that when I began to teach, I was in touch with Andrew, sharing what was happening with him. Even though I had stepped out of a formal relationship with him, I felt that to be in integrity I had to share what was occurring. When I was in the community, I was very close to him at some points, but I generally did not have a close personal relationship with him. Andrew encouraged and supported me to teach. I think that was very important to me. I don't know if I would have done it otherwise, because I was aware that even if my expression was different and I was diverging from the orientation of his teaching, in some ways I had to honor lineage and I was aware that if I'm going to teach, I have to be in integrity with my teacher, he has to be behind me. So, in that sense, you could say I'd left my teacher, but on a deeper level, the guru principle that transcended him as an individual was still very much there, and I knew I had to be true to that.

AMIR: How do you perceive the difference between you and your students? Specifically, is there a difference in what evolving means for you and what it means for your students?

PETER: The first thing that comes to mind is that there is no difference. I am not interested in being self-consciously in a role as teacher or creating any formal distance between myself and them. When I'm with them, some of them live here with us, I see them as the same as myself. It's interesting that we don't address them as our students. If someone asks, "Are you a student of Pete and Cynthia?" some of them will probably say yes, and some of them might not be so comfortable with it; it's just because it's not a terminology suitable for the structure of what we're doing. The fact is that of course they are, but

I think it speaks to a way we're doing this, which is not creating that kind of difference from the get-go and trying to find a way to enliven a context of verticality and natural hierarchy without getting stuck in unhealthy structures.

Obviously, when you meet a spiritual teacher who is clearly sitting up there in a way that implies, whether it's true or not, that they are completely consistent, that sets up something in the person coming to them right from the start: They are different, they are not me, they are extraordinary, etc. I think part of the interesting way we are going about it, which isn't really consciously contrived, is that we're just being who we are.

AMIR: Don't your not-students give you a certain mandate that they don't give each other?

PETER: Yes, for sure.

AMIR: So how is that different from the more traditional teacher-student model?

PETER: I say in nearly every group I'm in, that if there's anything I say or do that you are not sure about, you must say so. I'm always putting that responsibility on them, and if I'm teaching a retreat I'll always say, in some shape or form, "You don't need to believe what I'm saying, test in your own experience." I strongly emphasize that the foundation of what we are doing is inquiry and not belief. So I am trying to engender a healthy questioning, also of myself as teacher from the beginning. I also always say, in different ways, "Let's forget this notion of perfection, it doesn't exist in human beings, that's not the point." That creates a context in which people are maybe even able to trust in a way that they wouldn't if it was a traditional guru-disciple situation.

When I started doing this some years ago, I got an email from someone who was curious about what we are doing, because of what he saw about it on the internet. He asked, "In terms of how you're teaching, would you consider yourself a guru or a teacher, or are you what they call in Buddhism *kalyana mitta*, a spiritual friend?"

It was an interesting question for me, and I wrote back that I was in the middle somewhere. I said, "It's not really just a spiritual friend, where I'm on the path with you and only have a bit more experience. Something more dynamic, demanding and absolute is being shared, but it's not completely the other pole either." So this is what I'm interested in, some kind of new paradigm in between those two.

AMIR: Do you sometimes challenge students in a way that a friend wouldn't do, that only a spiritual teacher can do?

PETER: I think that, because of my experience of having been with a guru, and being cognizant of the benefits and importance of verticality, but also of the dangers, of which there are so many, there's sensitivity in me to what any individual is capable of, or would be appropriate at any moment, and obviously that is very tied to the personal relationship and depth of trust they have in me.

In terms of myself and the students, I have learned from mistakes when I was reluctant to make the vertical dimension of natural hierarchy clear, particularly with one person who was very bright and intellectually my peer, but he was also very proud. In the end when his superiority got confronted, he got very angry. I'll never forget it, because he said to me, "You are not my master!" He said that to me, and I replied, "Well, I never said I was. But you have chosen me as a teacher, you are here. So what about *natural* hierarchy, which you said you were interested in?" But he just kept saying, "You are not my master!" So our relationship broke down, which was very unfortunate, because he was a teacher himself, kind of an integral coach, and there were all the grounds for a very fruitful collaboration and relationship. He wanted something more, but he wasn't prepared to let go of his independence and control.

After that I realized that I had to make something more explicit in terms of the relationship with me, if people were going to get involved with me. After that, if someone new was interested in getting involved, either because they'd done the course or a long retreat with me, I would say, "If you're going to get involved, you need to give me the benefit of the doubt. You need to trust me fundamentally. Do you feel that you trust me fundamentally? Have we had enough interaction together?" Since then, the course has still been rocky, but something changed and something solidified in the group.

So now I test people to see if they are really interested in ego-transcendence and whether they fundamentally trust me before I take them on. It is a very fine line to walk and I am just finding my way with it. It is a huge and very challenging responsibility. I don't expect anyone to trust or to accept me as a teacher. But if that movement is authentically happening and I know I can catalyze and facilitate the awakening process in that individual, then I work with allowing that to happen while endeavoring to both make conscious of what they are choosing and to keep open a positive feedback loop. So there is a recognition and acceptance of the importance of trusting me and an acknowledgement on my part that I am also a work-in-progress, and that I welcome questioning. Also, most of my teaching work with committed students occurs in groups, not me in an explicit teacher position as I would be in a retreat or public talk situation. This means that the bigger view and liberation context is potentially communicated by many toward any individual and people tend to be able to trust more in the intelligence of the collective. So, in all these ways, I am working with natural hierarchy which is by definition always fluid. Sometimes I step forward and assert myself more explicitly as leader and teacher and sometimes I step back and take more of a facilitator role. I just feel into what wants to happen, into what is going to support the evolution of the whole and also of myself. It definitely keeps me on my toes!

These two interviews—with Saniel Bonder, to whom I was introduced through my work on this book, and Peter Bampton, my friend from our time together in Andrew's community—highlight an issue, that was absent from the traditional spiritual teacher-student relationship but that is very present in some of the twenty-first-century

Western versions of this relationship: the friction and even clash between mutuality and hierarchy in the teacher-student relationship.

As we know too well, the exclusively hierarchical model of the teacher-student relationship is fraught with perils, and nowadays many believe that in our postmodern era it is no longer relevant. Indeed, although most of the teachers I interviewed were initiated in a strictly, even absolutely, hierarchical teacher-student relationship, and acknowledge the benefits they gained from it, many of them, like Saniel and Peter, tend to accommodate the changing times or compensate for the shortcomings of that relationship model by shifting to a more egalitarian, only mildly hierarchical relationship model.

Nevertheless, as expressed by Saniel and Peter in these interviews and by many of the other interviewees in this book, it seems that the egalitarian-mutual approach also has serious shortcomings and may not serve well some of the goals of this relationship. This came out powerfully in Saniel's proclamation, "Devotion is a natural expression of my being; and in the situation we created, there wasn't really room for that to be naturally and fully expressed."

If the strictly hierarchical model no longer works for most students, and the model of assumed equality is, as is my feeling about it, a weak compromise, where do we go from here? The following conversation, I had with Thomas Steininger, points to a possible direction:

THOMAS STEININGER

AMIR: The question of hierarchy versus mutuality in the teacher-student relationship is related to something I discovered in some of my interviews, in which the teacher said that they needed their students in order to keep evolving spiritually. Some even went as far as to say that they were learning from the transaction just as much as the students were. My sense therefore is that the teacher-student relationship is not, as sometimes portrayed, a situation where a higher perspective or knowledge trickles through the teacher down to the student, but it's more complex and more reciprocal. The relationship itself is needed for both student and teacher to keep evolving.

THOMAS: That makes total sense to me. It's related to my understanding that the relationship process is the real teacher. The teacher is the teacher because they have a higher and more developed way of holding this process. The real thing is not about him or her, it's happening in the relationship and goes both ways. There is no equality because there is a difference in experience, depth, etc., but it's not a one-way street.

AMIR: What's important to notice here is that we're speaking about mutuality in a context that is hierarchical. I think that when Buber and other philosophers and teachers spoke about the meeting between individuals as the gateway to the absolute, the context is nonhierarchical. What I'm suggesting, and I think it's a somewhat unfamiliar concept, is that mutuality doesn't contradict hierarchy.

THOMAS: I completely agree. You can use a very obvious example, which is that between a father and his young son I would hope there is mutuality, but it would be damn wrong if it wasn't hierarchical. That seems to make it very clear that mutuality does not mean flatland.

CHAPTER 10
WHAT'S IN IT FOR THE TEACHER?

It is part of my happiness that many others should understand as I do, and that their understanding and desire should be entirely in harmony with my understanding and desire.

—**BARUCH SPINOZA**, *TREATISE ON THE EMENDATION OF INTELLECT*

One day we ourselves can step up to teaching. That doesn't necessarily mean we have to sit on a pulpit or be a spiritual teacher. But we could recognize that one of the best ways to keep learning is to teach. There is always somebody above us to learn from (speaking hierarchically, because it is simpler), and there is always somebody below us to teach, to pass it on to. So let's not always be on the receiving end. Let's also be on the giving end. I personally found that I grew more and learned more from my first three years of teaching around 1990 than if I had done a third three-year retreat in our cloistered Dzogchen center. Teaching and working with others, both with groups and with individuals, was really demanding. It pulled out the best of me. I learned a lot. I'd guess that the best college professors, just for example, are those who are really lifelong students with undimmed passion for their field. Therefore, let's respect the teacher principle in all of us, so we, too can eventually step up to that.

—**LAMA SURYA DAS**, *THE MIND IS MIGHTIER THAN THE SWORD*

CAROLYN LEE

In the introduction to the third edition of her spiritual teacher Adi Da's book, *The Knee of Listening*, Carolyn Lee wrote: "*The Knee of Listening* is an autobiography. It is the first-person account of the life of an unparalleled Spiritual Genius—alive today—whose appearance can only be rightly understood by referring to the tradition of the avatar, or the incarnations of the Divine." I interviewed Carolyn in order to explore with her the role that Adi Da's relationships with his closest students played in his life and teaching.

AMIR: A few days ago, I reflected on how fascinated I was, at the age of sixteen and seventeen, by the relationship between Jesus Christ and his disciples, which was quite unusual for a Jewish Israeli kid in the mid-'80s, and how this fascination was related to my current exploration of the teacher-student relationship.

CAROLYN: I am interested in what you are saying because when I was twelve years old, I was returning with my mother and my sister from the U.K. to Australia, and we stopped for a couple of days in Tel Aviv. This was in 1960, when Israel was very new. My mother, a protestant Christian, wanted to go to the main Christian holy places, but some of them were cut off by the pre-1967 border. One place we were able to go to was the Sea of Galilee. The Biblical stories about Jesus walking by the Sea of Galilee were so vivid to me there from all my Sunday school training. As I looked across the lake, I imagined the disciples in their fishing boats being called by Jesus. My mother, sister and I filled little bottles with water from the lake, which, from our point of view, was sacred. Then we went to the ruins of the town of Capernaum and visited the remains of the synagogue there, which is mentioned in the Gospels as a place where Jesus went. While wandering around the ruins, I fell over a stone and hit my big toe, resulting in a blood blister. I cherished this blister, which didn't go away for a long time. I was so proud of this tangible evidence of contact with these holy places.

My response was obviously coming from something more than a little bit of Sunday school. It was something very deep. What I feel about this question in your case and mine is that we are probably coming from past-life experiences of the master-disciple relationship—we're not just talking about our ideas or experiences in this lifetime.

AMIR: Well, to me, that's one possibility, and another possibility is that it's not as specific as past lives, but that we tap into what Jung called "the collective unconscious," which contains the master-disciple relationship, manifesting through some specific masters and their disciples. I guess the collective unconscious could be regarded as a version of past lives.

CAROLYN: I appreciate the way you just framed it, because you're pointing out that recognizing a master is more than a personal thing, it comes out of humanity's deep collective experience. In terms of this lifetime, I had no conscious interest in the master-disciple relationship at the time I encountered Bhagavan Adi Da. And I mean *zero* interest, apart from my Christian upbringing, which I had already given up. The way that Adi Da entered my life, so suddenly and overwhelmingly forcefully at a particular moment, is still one of the greatest mysteries, or, truly, *the* great mystery, of my life. It was totally a bolt out of the blue. Over the years, Adi Da spoke a lot about the supreme significance of the master-disciple relationship, or as he generally referred to it, the Guru-devotee relationship. He said that this relationship is the most ancient relationship, going back to pre-history, before human historical time. It is the process whereby human beings, becoming self-aware and asking questions about the meaning of life and death, would recognize unique beings who were able to do more than spin stories about what is true or not true, beings who could livingly transmit the power of the ultimate reality. This makes profound sense to me.

AMIR: I'd love to hear about your meeting with Adi Da and that bolt out of the blue.

CAROLYN: I first encountered Bhagavan Adi Da through his spiritual autobiography, *The Knee of Listening*, which was in its first edition when I first saw it back in 1984. My sister had already become Adi Da's devotee. She was younger than I was, and she had been a Tibetan Buddhist, following that practice for about ten years. I was a Roman Catholic at that point—part of my spiritual search had led me away from my Protestant upbringing, first through general agnosticism, then through Quakerism and then, probably because of my early devotional response to Jesus, I became a Catholic. I had no interest in Eastern religions, even though many spiritual seekers of my generation, including my sister, were inspired by Buddhism and so on. I, on the other hand, was very much a Westerner and, by that time, a scholar of medieval Christian music and liturgy. Nevertheless, when my sister showed me *The Knee of Listening*, my response was immediate. I opened the book and saw a picture of Adi Da on one side of the double opening, and on the other side, the beginning of the text, in which he was simply announcing himself, "I was born Franklin Albert Jones." It was utterly straightforward, and at the same time, in my experience, the most profound déjà vu. I was recognizing One I had always already known but never expected to find. Suddenly, everything was reframed. Everything that I felt about Jesus was now newly explicable. I intuitively understood that in my devotion to Jesus, I had been following some kind of residue, some trace in the being of the real master-disciple relationship. It was a total bolt out of the blue and I knew that I would have to pursue this with my life, whatever that involved.

It was 1984 and I was living in Ireland, I was married and I had an academic position in a university—there were all kinds of things to bind me to where I was. It took me two years to disentangle all of that. I left my marriage, my friends, my job, but the final thing that pushed me to this radical relinquishment of the whole structure of my life was seeing Bhagavan Adi Da in person.

That happened in the summer of 1986, when he came to Europe and sat in *darshan* (Sanskrit: sacred sighting of a Master) with devotees from all over Europe. His European devotees looked for a place where we could properly receive him, and found a former Catholic seminary in the south of Holland, which had a chapel large enough to accommodate everyone.

To this day, I recall the moment when Adi Da walked in and silently took possession of the space. There was no possibility, after that, to ever again see the world in the same way. He looked around the room, seeming to meet everyone's gaze, and yet there was no personal sense of him looking at me. It was rather that he consumed the room in the intensity of his regard. For the first time in my life, the physical reality became completely transformed, translucent. Not only was his form alight with a brilliance I had never seen before, but the whole space became that brilliance. In fact, there was no difference between him and the room. All of it appeared to arise in a radiance that had no origin in this world, and yet, was somehow the very substance of it.

What now began to happen was slow, timeless and profound. Various faces passed over his face—was this a Chinese Taoist Master, or an Indian sage, or a native American shaman? Was this the Christ painted on the walls? Or all of these and none of these? One half-sensed word arose for all of it: Glory. But nothing to do with "heaven." Rather, it was an exquisite, exalted rest, a root-knowing, an abiding in a free and deathless reality that had been there all the time, but never before revealed. I lost my sense of place in the room. I lost my sense of self. There was only the heart-certainty that this was the divine manifesting before my eyes.

A few months later, I went to Australia, because my sister was a member of Adi Da's community there, and the following year, in 1987, I went to California to join the Dawn Horse Press, the publisher of Adi Da's writings. Then, in 1994, I moved to Naitauba Island, Adi Da's Fijian hermitage, fulfilling my deepest desire, which was to live around him.

AMIR: I'm interested in your experience of living there, especially in how you see the role that the relationship between Adi Da and you, the disciples who lived there with him, played in the formulation of his teaching.

CAROLYN: From the beginning of his spiritual work, he emphasized that the foundation of his teaching is the relationship with him. He said, "I offer not a method, but a relationship." And that's the secret, you see. He said that there have been so many methods in the world aiming to help people find, or awaken to, what is ultimate, but all methods are founded on the efforts, the searches of the ego or the presumed separate self. In the master-disciple relationship, the seeking for what is ultimate falls away, because the deep heart-impulse to find what is true and real is answered, satisfied. The recognition of the divine in the form of the master awakens a love relationship and a devotional response that is unique and most profound. This recognition and the response that follows open the disciple to receive the master's spiritual transmission of his or her own state. And it is that transmission that transforms the disciple, not merely the practicing of a method. The master will also likely give practice instructions, but these are not the senior principle. The devotional relationship is the key that awakens the great process of spiritual realization. Adi Da would sometimes remark that we were asking him questions and he would appear to be responding at length to those questions, but the most important thing happening was that he was keeping us in the room with him, keeping us in the sphere of his transforming spiritual transmission.

AMIR: Would you say that keeping you in the room was also necessary for him to communicate and teach beyond the room?

CAROLYN: Absolutely. He sometimes talked about the "First Room." He would say that the room in which we were sitting with him was much, much more than the room that we were seeing from our point of view in space-time. He would say that the First Room is the limitless Room of Conscious Light, the absolute space, which includes everything and everyone. At the same time, he fully acknowledged that it was necessary for him to engage with individuals who came to him, in order to be able to reveal the body of his teaching. Nevertheless, all the while he was transmitting his state of Conscious Light, way beyond the room that we were aware of.

AMIR: When Adi Da answered people's questions, did you feel that his relationship with the person asking the question made a difference in how he would answer them?

CAROLYN: Yes. He made clear in many ways that it was not the question, but the questioner to which he was responding. A very similar question might be asked by two different people and the answers would be very different. His answer would have to do with where that person was coming from in terms of their own personality pattern and what the bondage was that needed to be understood and transcended. He also kept saying that ultimately, when there is a real awakening, the questions dissolve—but that the questions do have profound use, because it is not lawful for the master to give the sacred teaching casually. It must be respectfully requested. Those that feel the need for the grace of the teaching must draw it out of the master through their real questions and their willingness to adhere to the teaching.

AMIR: What I'm getting from what you're saying is that if one's relationship to the master was in a way removed or abstract, then they wouldn't draw the same kind of wisdom and depth of understanding from him, whereas devotion and love did do that.

CAROLYN: Absolutely right. In fact, sometimes, in response to a question, Adi Da would simply say, "Too intellectual." I sometimes received a critical response from him when I asked a question, and these occasions were always when I was coming from a mental place, rather than from real feeling and need. His whole body would change when he felt a question coming from a place that was, just like you said, one of genuine devotion.

AMIR: Could we say that the teacher needs there to be a relationship of love and devotion, because that enables the students to ask from a much deeper place in themselves?

CAROLYN: Exactly. And the sincere disciple is serving beings by exemplifying that right relationship to the master, and thus allowing him to give instruction that has universal truth and relevance.

What's in the teacher-student relationship for the *student* seems in-tuitively clear enough: the student wants the teacher to guide them in their spiritual journey; they want the teacher to facilitate their spiritual awakening, or help them get established in an awakened state; they want the teacher to catalyze their mental and spiritual development and maturation; they want the teacher to help them overcome or remove their inner blockages and obstacles, and support their blooming in their full potential; and so on.

But what's in it for the teacher? Why do they want to teach? What do they need the student for? What spiritual benefits do they receive from the student? The answers to these questions were much less clear to me when I started this exploration into the teacher-student relationship, and I posed them to many of the teachers I interviewed.

One benefit for the teacher, highlighted in the above interview with Carolyn Lee, is especially relevant when it is assumed that the teacher's awakening or spiritual development is complete. Carolyn expressed it in saying about her teacher, Adi Da, that "it was neces-sary for him to engage with individuals who came to him, in order to be able to reveal the body of his teaching." In other words, in such a case the teaching enables the teacher to reveal the knowledge, or activate capacities and potentials, that are *already* in them but would not have been revealed or activated otherwise.

Another benefit, which came out in other interviews, is relevant when the teacher continues to be seen as "work in progress." In such a case, working with students, caring for them and aspiring to be-come a more skilled and effective facilitator of their spiritual growth, inspires and challenges the teacher to keep developing. This devel-opment is not seen as restricted, in any way, to the teacher "func-tion," but applies to their entire being. We could say that, in such a case, the teacher *needs* the students to continue his or her spiritual journey.

But not necessarily so. We will end this chapter with an important and provocative comment, made by Vipassanā teacher Christopher Titmuss, that whether being in a teaching position is psycho-spiritually beneficial or disadvantageous for the teacher entirely depends on the individual and is far from a given.

CHRISTOPHER TITMUSS

AMIR: In an interview with another teacher a few days ago, I asked him what spiritual benefits he was receiving from being a teacher, and he said, "It forces me to be a channel to a knowledge that is not my own. Sometimes, in a teaching situation, I get asked a question that I have no idea how to answer, and then I hear myself give the exactly right answer for that person in that situation. I'm amazed by what comes of my mouth." Does that happen to you?

CHRISTOPHER: Insights emerge in a variety of ways, and this dynamic can take place in any kind of exchange, not only between teacher and student. It can happen, for example, in a group when people share together, in meditation, in solitude and in the nature. These are all invaluable resources for insight. What may be unique to a teacher sharing wisdom or understanding to a group of students is that the voice of insight can simultaneously benefit the individual student, the whole group and the teacher at the same time.

AMIR: So being in the teacher's position demands from the teacher that he or she respond with clarity and care to the person they are speaking with, while being very aware of what's appropriate and beneficial for the whole group.

CHRISTOPHER: In my forty years as a Dharma teacher, I have invited more than a hundred teachers to teach with me on retreats and various gatherings, and I also attended talks of many other teachers. My impression is that many teachers just keep repeating their talks and responses, and I don't get the picture of any insight emerging through such repetition. In fact, the mind of some teachers only gets smaller and more dogmatic as they teach, and they just give almost the exact same talk every time with the same answers. So it's definitely not the case for everyone.

CHAPTER 11

THE PRICE OF REVELATION

It is common opinion among us in regard to beauty and wisdom that there is an honorable and a shameful way of bestowing them. For to offer one's beauty for money to all comers is called prostitution; but we think it virtuous to become friendly with a lover who is known to be a man of honor. So is it with wisdom. Those who offer it to all comers for money are known as sophists, prostitutors of wisdom.

—SOCRATES TO ANTIPHON IN *MEMORABILIA*

How can a vocation be put on a payroll? How is it possible to price revelation? The question has haunted me and left me uneasy during my whole life as a teacher. Why have I been remunerated, given money, for what is my oxygen and raison d'etre?... By what oversight or vulgarization should I have been paid to become what I am? When, and I have felt this with sharpening malaise, it might have been altogether more appropriate for me to pay those who invited me to teach?

Irate, derisive common sense cries out: teachers must live, even those high Masters, whom you probably romanticize, must eat! So many of them already suffer a wretched lot. To which unanswerable challenge an imp of the perverse, in an idiom not altogether of this world, murmurs: "Living and eating are indeed absolute necessities, but also bleak and secondary in the light of the exploration and communication of the great and final

things." Are there no alternatives to the professionalization, to the mercan-
tilization of the Master's calling, to the equivalence between truth-seeking
and salary introduced by the Sophists?

—GEORGE STEINER, *LESSONS OF THE MASTERS*

In the decade since I left Andrew Cohen's community, I have been deeply involved in various activities, that brought my spiritual-philosophical search and inquiry into the public arena—co-founding the Israeli Education Spirit movement and serving as its managing director, co-leading dozens of "contemplative pedagogy" projects, organizing and participating in "collective self-inquiry" groups, etc. As a matter of principle (with few exceptions), I did not ask for or accept money for any of these activities. My rationale was, and remains, that since I can make a living as a medical translator (which I have been doing successfully for the last thirty years), I prefer not to mix activities, that have to do with my soul and spirit, with issues related to money making and livelihood.

To my wife and close friends, this makes no sense, and they keep bringing up the issue with me: Why aren't you turning your philosophical-spiritual inquiry into a source of income? Why are you insisting on separating your livelihood from what you care about and interested in the most? Why continue doing work that brings you no joy, while you can make money by doing something you like and enjoy?

Their arguments make sense to me, yet something in me—my heart? Spirit? Self-image? Spiritual ego?—gets all squeamish and uncomfortable whenever I consider charging money for "skills" I developed in my spiritual journey and for what I have been doing my whole life as a "hobby," albeit one that has been the focal point of my life.

From these personal questions, I began exploring the question of whether it was appropriate for a spiritual teacher to charge their students money for their teachings. This is an age-old question, going all the way back to fifth century B.C. Greece, when the early sophists' provided wisdom only to those who could pay, which earned them Socrates' scorn and condemnation. Nowadays, although charging money (and sometimes large sums) for retreats, workshops and personal consultation has become the norm for spiritual teachers, that question has not gone away. It came up, for example, in my interview with integral philosopher-activist and spiritual teacher Terry Patten, founder of Integral Spiritual Practice.

TERRY PATTEN

TERRY: I think that there are a lot of very bad ideas that have a great deal of power and currency in the current spiritual marketplace. Ideas like "intellectual property" and the "productizing" of spiritual teachings. What we now see is a spiritual marketplace in which the student is a consumer and the teacher is a producer. This completely subverts the traditional sacred teacher-student relationship. There are many problems with the way money functions in the marketplace, which are not acknowledged or understood. To the degree that the student is the consumer in a dynamic where "the customer is king," the preferences of the separate self, or ego, rule. That's profoundly unhealthy. Wisdom then becomes a commodity, while of course it's not, so wisdom goes underground. The "fee for services" model is an unacknowledged shadow of the whole transformational industry. It's a huge problem.

AMIR: How do you think it should ideally work?

TERRY: The purity of the teacher-student relationship is a love relationship. You fall in love with your student, you see their divinity, and this becomes your overwhelming motivation. You are totally committed to their transformation. But the teacher can't practically enact that model. How can he or she act on the presumption of being in love with his or her students entirely for free? There needs to be a value exchange if the teacher is to survive and thrive. So the teacher becomes a producer of a service the student purchases.

In the absence of a better business model, I offer services for a fee. Thus, I've opened my heart and extended myself to students and then, when they didn't re-enroll in my offerings, I haven't maintained my relationship with them. On a spiritual level, that's painful. It doesn't feel right. My impulse is to keep presuming relationships and to stay committed to each of them. I think of them, but I don't have time to engage them in depth. I don't see a practical way to embody the kind of commitment that our spiritual connection implies, which is a no-matter-what commitment. I haven't yet found a simple clean way to transcend those unhealthy market dynamics, and that bugs me.

I explored this question further with several other teachers, and the following are excerpts from my interviews with Mooji (Chapter 8) and with Llewellyn Vaughan-Lee (Chapter 3). Each of them holds a clear position in relation to this "money for teaching" question— and their positions are markedly different.

MOOJI

AMIR: There seem to be people who think that money and spiritual transmission don't go well together, that bringing money into the picture somehow casts a shadow over the teacher's work. What is your view on this?

MOOJI: Let's go back to basics: What do we mean by spirituality, money and the use of money? I take spirituality to mean that which enables you to escape a life of delusion, of ignorance, of suffering, by guiding your mind back to its source, the pure Self, or Heart, which is also another name for God. The seeker practices or puts into effect the guidance received from a teaching or a teacher until the seeming obstacles to the realization of the Truth cease to exist. All of this we call spirituality.

Now, let's look at money. I see money as a great invention of God. There is something beautifully clean about money. Basically, it's like a courteous impersonal agreement, meaning we can trade with one another without having to please or manipulate each other. You give me this item or service and I give you this in exchange, whether it be shells or precious stones or what is presently called "money" all over the world. The universal impulse to trade or exchange is a way of life and is as old as time.

We have to be clear that money in itself isn't a bad thing. One cannot put a price on Truth or on the teaching of Truth. Truth cannot be sold. It is even beyond value, because it is the source of all things. This is not an easy thing to convey or grasp; nevertheless, it is the truth, and we must confirm this through experience. Money and spirituality don't go together only in the minds of those who believe this, because one can choose anything and say it doesn't go together with spirituality. For example, some people think that spirituality and relationships don't go together, or spirituality and living in a city don't go together, or whatever else from a wide array of things your mind struggles against. Money does not tarnish spirituality. Nothing can cast a shadow over the pure teachings—only greed and one's inner attitude can. How could money corrupt or be corrupted in itself? Money is not sentient. It doesn't decide to belong to you. If there is any corruption, it is in the mind of the perceiver or the desirer.

AMIR: If it's that simple, how do you explain the fact that so many teachers exploited their students?

MOOJI: In my view, these are not true teachers and definitely not teachers of Truth. If your heart is not aligned with Truth, consciousness will not support you and your activities for long. If there is a greed or craving for money, or any attachment or desire for the power or respect that money seems to promise, then I can see how it all becomes a big mess. But in so many cases, money that flows towards an ashram or temple or any other spiritual establishment is used to good effect. For example, they provide an environment where seekers can study and contemplate the teachings of a liberated being, or they make the teaching available through the internet to seekers all over the world who would not otherwise be able to participate. Many of them also support other causes either individually or collectively working to raise the level of consciousness in the human kingdom.

AMIR: Still, it is usually money, sex or lust for power that makes people lose their balance and create big messes. So there is something about money, and especially about connecting money with spiritual seeking.

MOOJI: Something in the conditioned mind singles out money. There is an emotional element to people's judgment that says that to associate money with Truth shows a falsehood straight away. But I find such views to be deeply naïve and unjustified, arising largely from ignorance. Money is simply a tool that can be used for the expansion and sharing of spirituality, particularly in the age of information technology. For one who is established in the heart, money is another ingenious expression of consciousness and in harmony with God's expression as life. It is mind that creates the sense of a problem, and specifically the ego-mind steeped in personhood. Money is only of value when it is in flow or service. People spend money not just on necessities like food but on momentary pleasures, such as entertainment, drugs and alcohol. Spirituality increases the quality of your life and brings you to a place much greater than anything you have spent money on in this world. Would it not be an act of compassion if while investing in your own awakening, you simultaneously support the movement for universal awakening?

This notion of not mixing money and spirituality is also a cultural attitude that is prevalent more in the west. In India, for example, which is a nation that cultivates and venerates spirituality, liberation, Truth and God, people have a completely different approach. They give openly and from the heart to what they value most, and they take care of their religious and spiritual traditions and establishments. It's a fantasy more in some Western minds that money has no place in spirituality, as though what is needed should just fall out of the sky—and sometimes it does, but it is not my consistent experience. Some people are too stuck in images such as Jesus preaching on the Mount of Olives with everybody sitting around in hundreds, leaning against stones, without microphones or speakers or central-heated halls. We're in a different time now, and the spiritual hunger around the world is also greater than ever before. There was a time when seekers had to expend a lot of energy and money just to find a spiritual master, who was often in a remote place. The grace of technology brings seekers to teachers who may not be in their physical presence and they can benefit in real time and just as powerfully by tuning in from their own homes.

AMIR: You are describing a very positive function for money in the teacher-student relationship.

MOOJI: I feel that for true teachers, or awakened beings, money is not personally important. But if their presence commands an interest and respect from seekers who clearly want to spend time with them, and the interest and demand grows, then at some point, some form of organization needs to spring up into action in order to facilitate this. Who would cover the costs that arise to share teachings of Truth on a global scale? Shouldn't the ones attending retreats and seminars contribute? If the seekers all live in your village, that's fine. You can meet in the garden, and each person then goes back to their own home. But, say, some from other countries want to see you, must you pay for their flight tickets? Where do we draw the line, and what exactly should be free in terms of this spiritual cliché that spirituality should be free? Truth *is* free, spirit *is* free, and they bring freedom, but in order to make the teachings accessible in the modern world, it is unrealistic to envision doing so without the aid of money. I don't think God has a problem with money.

AMIR: What role did money play in your own development as a teacher?

MOOJI: In the early days of having satsang gatherings in the U.K., I could not meet people in my little flat for long as the numbers of people who wanted to come grew very quickly. When looking for somewhere to meet, I found that everything cost money—even the church hall across from my house had a high rental fee; they didn't care that we were sharing Truth. So I was selling chai and incense on the street to make the money to rent a hall to make the gatherings free for such beings. I learned that even if the people renting spaces like you very much, they will still charge you the full rental fee. It is just the nature of life if certain expressions are to unfold to their full potential—spiritual or otherwise—and there is nothing wrong with that.

Many years have passed since those early days and still my whole teaching is available without charge to everyone who desires it. Hundreds of thousands of seekers embark upon and deepen in their spiritual journeys through the internet, such as watching videos on YouTube and other media platforms. Our largest and perhaps most important event is the One Sangha Gathering, where many hundreds of people come for free in terms of food, accommodation and satsang. But without the support of donations or some other retreats which have a charge, it is difficult to continue to work in this way and to continue producing an abundance of free material for everyone. There's a lot going on that people don't see. We now live in a very rural and remote place and there was no internet when we first arrived; it was raw land, without electricity or running water. We had to buy the service and lines to have internet to share satsang and free videos with people around the world, and so that now, paradoxically, some of them can come back to complain about why not everything is free.

AMIR: So how do you relate to people's complaints?

MOOJI: I came across this saying: "Nobody becomes poor by giving." This is a wonderful saying and observation. It comes from wisdom. People give their love, their patience and energy, generously and over-abundantly. They're giving in service. Why is money singled out and scrutinized? Money is sometimes the easiest thing to give, while others are giving blood, sweat and tears for what they love, trust and believe in.

Charging for spirituality has been a big excuse that the mind has somehow developed as a distraction from Truth. I don't think it is a genuine concern. There are often some seeds of bitterness inside certain beings that cause them to project onto others in this way. If one has really received the fruits of satsang in the heart, a gratitude arises. If you find something which brings joy and peace to your life and to those around you, don't you find it is natural to want to give something back to support it out of love and appreciation? It doesn't even need to be money—your blessing and goodwill is also a beautiful support. Those who speak negatively must not have received, for if they had, they could not put a value on what they are discovering.

AMIR: Don't you ever hear such remarks from any of your students?

MOOJI: They wouldn't be my true students. They could only be people who lack the courage to be free. We must turn the lamp around to look at the ones with these concepts about money, for we would find many inconsistencies. In the early days of satsang, some people came forward saying they couldn't afford to come to a retreat and I would always accommodate them. Then, during one retreat, I found out that some of those very people were secretly smoking marijuana on the retreat. They had money to buy marijuana but not to pay for satsang! It also became evident that some were not valuing what they were receiving because it didn't cost them anything. I find when people pay for something, they often treat it with greater importance. I guess they don't like to feel they are wasting their money or time.

AMIR: Would you say that personally for you the question of money-for-spiritual-guidance is not a real issue?

MOOJI: Ultimately, I look at all of this just as a play of consciousness for each one to check in to find what is true and to transcend small-mindedness and all misconceptions about who we are and how life should be lived. I don't take anything of this world so seriously or personally. For me, it is all consciousness dancing. I have a joy in watching those who are called to search for Truth find it. This is where my heart is called to serve. I don't have much interest in talking about people who are looking at your shoelaces and asking where you got the money from to buy them. I share all this now for the sake of those who may have genuine misunderstandings or doubts about the association of money and spirituality, to clarify that their thinking is not correct. I invite them to drop their concepts about such things and to instead focus on coming to a higher place of seeing. Yes, there are, and will continue to be, people who exploit others for their own gain—like it or not, these things are a part of life too. But don't let them distract or stop you from searching for what is true, because Truth never becomes a lie, and the lie never becomes true.

Put your full attention on liberating your mind and enjoy this dream of consciousness while being awake. The Truth that you are is so magnificent. Don't get stuck on these things that keep your attention fixated upon the fleeting things of this world. Leave all these completely aside now, even for just a moment—a true moment of consciousness being fully aware of itself—and wake up to who you are: the timeless and imperishable Self.

LLEWELLYN VAUGHAN-LEE

LLEWELLYN: The essence of the Sufi path is the transmission of grace, or love, that is given through the chain of succession from teacher to disciple. This spiritual energy, or grace, is given either individually or at group meditation meetings. As grace by its very nature is free, a divine gift, there can never be a charge for these meetings or this transmission—otherwise the energy will become subtly corrupted.

I come from a very traditional Sufi background, and we were taught that money can never be charged for meditation. I never have any direct financial relationship with my students. They are left completely free. However, my teacher said that if you have learned something with your mind, then you can charge. So for example when I give a seminar and discuss Sufi teachings which I have learned and studied, then I can charge. But for meditation, or private guidance, it is just grace that is given, so there can be no charge.

There is also the danger that if you charge you can become financially dependent upon students, and thus the freedom that is an essential quality of spiritual work, becomes lost. It is also so easy to be drawn to give the student what they want, rather than what they need—to teach feel-good spirituality rather than the real path to liberation, the real way to divine love and oneness, which is often hard and painful. The teacher must be free if he or she is to guide the student to inner freedom.

CHAPTER 12
SURRENDER AND AUTONOMY

Autonomy as popularly conceived is a kind of self-deception. It may protect against false spiritual authority, but it also protects and preserves the seeker's false ego-self. Paradoxically, the true autonomy of the seeker's intrinsic being develops out of surrender to genuine spiritual authority.

—KEN WILBER, *SPIRITUAL CHOICES*

For the mature disciple it should not even matter, in principle, whether or not the teacher is fully awakened. Obedience is simply a means of actively demonstrating the self-transcending disposition that is crucial to spiritual life.

—GEORG FEUERSTEIN, *HOLY MADNESS*

There is no such thing as a good influence, Mr. Gray. All influence is immoral—immoral from the scientific point of view.

Why?

Because to influence a person is to give him one's own soul. He does not think his natural thoughts, or burn with his natural passions. His virtues are not real to him. His sins, if there are such things as sins, are borrowed. He becomes an echo of someone else's music, an actor of a part that has not been written for him. The aim of life is self-development. To realize one's nature perfectly—that is what each of us is here for.

—OSCAR WILDE, *THE PICTURE OF DORIAN GRAY*

While I was working on this book, and about half a year after having my first interview with my former teacher Andrew Cohen, I received from him the following email:

> *Dear Amir,*
>
> *I hope you are well.*
>
> *Someone just forwarded me the interview you did with Tomer Persico and I wanted to clear up what may be some misunderstanding between us with regards to why I called you back to Foxhollow. It was only for one reason: After all those years as my student, you finally were strong and independent enough to become a core player in our work. I was honoring what I saw in your development and wanted to give you the opportunity to engage with me and other core students in a way you had not been prepared to do up until that point. I was not trying to deprive you of anything, quite the opposite. Remember, rightly or wrongly, my priorities were always focused on developing our core body. Its strength and depth would be the strength and depth of our movement and our work. I wanted you to participate at a deeper level at that point. I don't say this to justify the wrong choice to close the center, but simply to help you to know what I was thinking at the time.*
>
> *I am happy to discuss any of this for clarification if you would like.*
>
> *Sending Love,*
> *Andrew*

The email caught me completely by surprise. The interview Andrew was referring to was one I gave three years earlier, in July 2013, to the Israeli scholar Tomer Persico, for his two-part article, "Andrew Cohen and the Decline of the Guru Institution," published in Israeli Maariv newspaper on July 26, 2013. When asked about the circumstances in which I left Andrew, after being his student for more than twenty years, I replied:

> *At the time I was co-managing the center in Israel, and I decided that if we really wanted to contribute to the development of the society and culture [in the country], then we have to go out and get involved with what was happening in the society and culture, rather than keep busy only with our small center in Jaffa. The moment I started doing that, I started flourishing. Initially, to my surprise, Andrew supported me in that endeavor but at some point he must have decided that I and the Israeli center were becoming too independent, and to put a stop to that. At that point I started doubting his motives and developed an increasing sense of grievance towards him. Then, while I was visiting the community's world center in the U.S.A., he called me for a meeting and told me that he had decided to close the center in Israel and that he wanted me to return to the U.S. and be part of the "core group" around him. At that moment something broke within me. I knew that he was completely wrong and that I shouldn't acquiesce—that complying with his instruction would mean I would be betraying myself and all the people I had developed connections with in Israel. Suddenly the magic was gone. As soon as I said "no" to him, I ceased regarding him as my teacher. I returned to Israel as a "free man" and although I went through a lot of pain as a result of leaving him and all my spiritual comrades, who had comprised my entire world for the last twenty years, I was in no doubt that I was doing the right thing. Everything that has happened since then showed me that I was right.*

While contemplating how to respond to Andrew's email, I decided that, although I wasn't sure that I could trust his memory of his motivation at the time that I left him, I would take it at face value, and use it to explore the clash between surrender and autonomy. I suggested to Andrew that we have another interview, dedicated to the paradox of autonomy and surrender in general and specifically as it manifested in his relationships with his teacher and with me, as his student. Our second interview took place via Skype.

ANDREW COHEN

AMIR: Andrew, you had several teachers before you met your guru, H.W.L. Poonja. How was he different from them?

ANDREW: It was a completely different relationship. For example, sometime after I started practicing Vipassana I met a teacher named Christopher Titmuss, who was the only Western Buddhist teacher I had sat with who seemed to have a spark of liberated consciousness. He seemed to carry the fragrance of liberation in a way that none of the other Buddhist meditation teachers that I met did. He would laugh spontaneously... I fell in love with him, admired him and was very devoted to him. He gave me a lot of confidence in the practice and in the path, which was enormously beneficial to me. But even though I found him the most compelling of all the Buddhist teachers, I never thought of him as formally my teacher.

Finding your real guru is not like going to a yoga teacher, a karate teacher or a meditation teacher. A good teacher, who is well trained, can share with you both the theory and practice of their particular method, but a guru shows you who you are simply through their very being. The most famous ashram in Rishikesh, in northern India, is the Shivananda Ashram. In the front office, there is a sign on the wall. It says, "Teaching means Being."

AMIR: And that's what you felt when you met him?

ANDREW: Initially, I didn't realize who he really was. He kept referring to himself as "Master," and I kept wondering, why is this old man who is dressed in shabby clothes, living in a small upstairs bedroom in his son's house, always calling himself the Master? Why did all his guests come and touch his feet before they sat down respectfully in front of him? I spent three weeks with him, both mornings and afternoons, going for walks, sharing meals and constantly asking him questions. Sometimes I thought this was the most extraordinary person I'd ever met, and other times, I thought he was just a crazy old man.

But something was definitely happening to me in his presence. One thing that comes to my mind is that, a few days after I met him, we were in his room, he was sitting on his bed and I was sitting on the chair next to him, when suddenly, out of the blue, I heard myself utter out loud the words: "I want to die but I don't know how." I was completely surprised when I said it. It came out of me without any premeditation. It didn't come from my ego or my mind. He seemed to recognize the metaphysical significance of what was happening, and his eyes filled with tears. So, through meeting this man I came to the point of profound surrender and submission, of giving up completely. This was a direct experience of Jesus' famous declaration, "not my will but Thy will be done."

Just before I left him, vowing to return a month later, he stated with utter confidence, "Pay attention. Something very big is going to happen to you." And he wasn't wrong. Shortly after I left him, my whole being exploded in ecstasy. A current of energy and consciousness literally overwhelmed my whole being. At times, it felt like I was being crushed by it. My heart was aching unbearably and ecstatically.

It was only then that I realized who he really was, not just his human form or personality but who he *really* was. Then I knew he was my *Master*, my guru forever. I realized he was an incarnation of God in human form, a living source through which the absolute principle manifests in this world. When you are lucky enough to have had that kind of extraordinary experience, you begin to worship the form of the Master, the human being, because of the immeasurable role they have played in your liberation.

AMIR: If I remember the story correctly, he didn't really want you to stay with him.

ANDREW: No. In fact, he said to me, "I have taught you everything I have to teach. Don't rely on me for anything. Stand on your own two feet." He made it clear that I had been given everything. Now in retrospect I can see that, even though the gift had been given in my hand, I *wanted* to have a guru-disciple, parent-child, father-son relationship with him, with the man who was my guru. I wanted a personal connection with him.

Then, after I started teaching, when I returned to India to visit him, I felt that something was wrong in our relationship. I said to him, "Master, is something wrong? I feel you are distant." And he just said, "How can I possibly be distant?" After that, every time that I went to see him there was something in me that was desperately seeking, wanting, yearning for a human relationship with him, and I was uncomfortable, I felt ill at ease, because the personal connection wasn't there anymore. But he just knew that the personal relationship between us was over, because it had served its function.

AMIR: Where there other ways in which Poonjaji pushed you to become independent, to stand on your own two feet?

ANDREW: He kept telling me that I was the greatest, that I was incredible, that I was God's gift to humanity. My understanding of that now is that through encouraging me to believe in myself absolutely, he intended for me to be a thoroughly fit vehicle through which Absolute Spirit could be powerfully transmitted. His showering me with praise was from his point of view, a radical psychotherapy, getting me to give up any doubt in myself that had yet to be eradicated. During this process, one day, I told him I was experiencing self-doubt and fear, to which he responded with the most ferocious intensity, screaming at the top of his lungs, "Never, *ever* doubt yourself!"

He wanted my belief in myself to be unshakable, and the incredible confidence that he bestowed in me made it possible for me, in the early years, when I was teaching and functioning as a guru, to see and respond to what was happening around me so much faster than my mind could comprehend. I would be seeing things and responding like an expert marksman, again and again hitting the bull's eye. It was all happening at the speed of light and that was because I'd let go so deeply. I was trusting so much. I trusted my gut implicitly, and that made me very, very effective. It was the grace of my Guru at work. It really works. People were compelled, attracted and deeply inspired.

AMIR: Did the difference you initially felt between you and Poonjaji disappear at some point?

ANDREW: In my experience, the guru or the form of the guru was and is *always* recognized to be higher than oneself. At a nondual level, at the deepest level, there is no difference—there is only One. But in the world of form, in the world of multiplicity and duality, the Guru should never be seen as equal to oneself.

AMIR: Why is that?

ANDREW: Because the guru represents God or the Absolute, that which is Highest, the Ultimate Truth, our own liberated hearts. In the world of duality, our puny human small self could never be equal to *that*.

Even after I became a teacher, with students of my own all over the world, the minute I got near him, I spontaneously would fall into a position of submission and reverence to him. It was because of who he had been for me and who he was. Indeed, in a dualistic context, being near his physical presence would always be the closest I could be to the Presence of God. Now when I see his image, even on a YouTube video, I don't see the man. I mean, I see the man, but even now he represents Absolute Spirit to me. So I can never see him as only a human being. He still represents the unreachable, unimaginable, inconceivable nature of spirit.

AMIR: This is also how we, your older students, related to you. How did you feel about that at the time?

ANDREW: In the early years of my teaching, we were practicing Guru Yoga. The idea behind it, which comes from India, is that the human form, the personality of the guru, is filled up and animated by nondual, infinite consciousness, making it possible for him or her to transmit this consciousness to other people. The form of the guru then is also worshiped as an expression of God or as a portal to the divine. That was my experience with my own teacher, and because people were having similarly strong experiences in my presence, they began to worship my form. I didn't ask them to, but it was happening spontaneously and I surrendered to it. At the time, I thought that was part of what I needed to do. I willingly performed that role for at least the first ten or fifteen years of my teaching career. It was implicit and while I would never do it again, in many ways, at the time, it was working.

AMIR: Worship of the guru's form is one aspect of Guru Yoga. Can you speak about other aspects of it?

ANDREW: I heard the great Swami Chidananda once say, "If you don't have a guru to help you correct your faults, to show you your pride, selfishness and ego-based motives, who will have the courage to show you the error of your ways?" Traditionally, that's what the guru does. He or she helps you to see yourself in a way no one else would ever dare to do.

When I became a guru, I saw this function as part of my role for those who had chosen me to be their teacher. This meant that at times, I was brutally honest with people about their shortcomings. Some people deeply appreciated this and found it helpful and liberating. Others at times were offended. It's complicated. When is it most helpful to tell someone the truth about themselves? When is it an insensitive and destructive thing to do? I've certainly done both. Now that I'm older and wiser, I'm definitely choosing to err on the side of caution. That means, that these days most of the time I choose to keep my mouth shut.

AMIR: Is part of the Guru Yoga, in your eyes, the student's trust that, when it comes to their spiritual, psychological and moral development, the teacher always knows better than them?

ANDREW: The foundation of this practice is that if you want to experience a freedom that is profound beyond measure, at some point, you have to be willing to trust the teacher more than you trust yourself. This means, at least for a limited period of time, you must be willing to give up unquestioned belief in the conclusions of your own unenlightened mind and to trust your own conviction in the higher knowledge and awakened intelligence of the teacher. When you are willing to trust in this way, you (at least temporarily) are letting go of your own already-knowing mind and are daring to embrace a rare state of vulnerability and receptivity to the awakened teacher's transmission of spiritual freedom.

When this process works, there is a profound and transformative result with deep and lasting consequences. That being said, the problem is, in this unique context, you are often asked not only to give up your own already-knowing mind, but at the same time, you are unknowingly asked to give up your own authority and subvert your independent discrimination. Implicitly and explicitly, you are required to conform to the conclusions and beliefs of the teacher. And also, for most people, their ego wants to be affirmed, to be seen in a favorable light by the teacher. This problem may result in you unknowingly being corrupted by your own fear of displeasing the teacher. In this context, inevitably too many people end up selling themselves out, giving up their own power, autonomy and independence.

In the traditional mythic context, unconditional submission to spiritual authority makes sense. In the postmodern context, however, submitting your natural authority, your capacity to discriminate and ultimately your right to be yourself, makes no sense and will never work. In the long run, it will almost inevitably inhibit your innate, unique capacity to evolve and develop in your own way, in your own time. Important dimensions of your own mind and soul are subverted when you submit to conformity. You become infantilized and your development is stunted.

That being said, unless at least for a *period of time* we can surrender unconditionally and absolutely our own mind and *even* our own will, we will never make it to the yonder shore.

AMIR: Do you see any way out of this dilemma?

ANDREW: The only way I see is that the contract between the teacher and the student has to be founded upon absolute responsibility and complete freedom of the student from the very beginning and at all times. The contract would require the teacher to *always* respect a student's boundaries, innate capacities and level of interest. This would leave *both* the teacher and the student free and unencumbered.

AMIR: Such responsibility has to be based on quite a high level of maturity and independence of the student, which you can expect from people after ten or twenty years on the path but which is very rare to find when people just get on the path.

ANDREW: What you're saying is true, but maybe if a student were to accept self-responsibility from the very beginning, it would demand of them a level of seriousness that would compel them to carry on their shoulders the burden of their own karma and spiritual development, and greatly facilitate their development.

AMIR: I'd like to explore with you now the question of individuation in the context of spiritual development, and start with the question—do you see individuation as a psychological and cultural need, that has to be respected, or is there such a thing as spiritual individuation?

ANDREW: The spiritual force, the spiritual current, is impersonal. It doesn't need to individuate. But you as an evolving individual, when you reach the postmodern stage of development, need to individuate. What's driving that need to individuate is the current of evolution itself. In other words, individuation is a process of complexification driven by the evolutionary impulse. Therefore, this process is both psychological-cultural *and* driven by the force of spirit itself.

AMIR: And on a personal level—do you see, for example, your separation from Poonjaji in 1991, or whenever the ultimate breakup happened, as part of your spiritual individuation? Was it necessary for you to become autonomous, independent of him, in order to pave your own unique spiritual path?

ANDREW: Yes, undoubtedly. Because, aside from any other reason for the complexity in our relationship, for me to develop my own, different interpretation of enlightenment, and to find its expression as an original teaching, that breakup needed to happen.

AMIR: Your experience with your teacher, as well as with your students, seems to indicate that surrender and autonomy clash with each other, and may even be incompatible.

ANDREW: Yes, it does seem this way. Which is why, as I've been saying, the new unbreakable law has to be that the autonomy of the individual must be fully honored and respected in every moment, no matter what. This has to be one of the new golden rules and, theoretically, the experience of unconditional surrender should be possible in the context of an individual, who never had to or was never allowed to give up their autonomy.

AMIR: I'm relating what you're speaking about to my experience with you, and what you're suggesting, then, is that the kind of surrender I, for example, experienced with you, does not necessarily or inherently demand giving up autonomy in any way.

ANDREW: That's right. Because the surrender is to Spirit, to what the Guru represents and transmits, and not to the man. So it does not depend on imagining the Guru to be some kind of a perfected human being, who always sees everything clearly and is never wrong. Actually, I've come to realize that the mythic posture of the Guru is completely co-created. It's not real. It's an artifice.

AMIR: I don't know if I thought you were perfect or even always saw things clearly—actually, I'm sure I didn't. But since you were representing Spirit, or that which is beyond me as an individual, and expressing motives that were beyond my small-self motives, in practical terms, surrendering to that which is beyond me meant surrendering to you and to those motives. And the clash between that surrender and my process of individuation is what ultimately caused the breakup of our relationship in 2009. I think it would be interesting to look at the email you recently wrote me in that context.

ANDREW: I'd be happy to. I'll start by saying that, at the time, I had a particular formula, which was that the structure of the inner body of students was the core of our work—and I want to emphasize "our" because it wasn't "mine," but "ours"—and everything was secondary to that. So from my point of view at the time, because you became much stronger and independent, and suddenly had the capacity to engage with me at a level that I had never seen in you before, I wanted you to be close to me and be a core player in our work.

Now, in retrospect, I realize I was probably wrong. Had I allowed people to individuate, find their own creative expressions of the work, had I honored it instead of trying to control it, I'm sure the teachings would have blossomed and developed in different ways. But I didn't have the eyes to see it at the time.

AMIR: The way I see it, what was happening for me at that point was that my process of becoming strong and independent was clashing with my surrender and obedience to you, or to the "us," which you saw yourself as representing. Another way of looking at it is that there was a clash between my needs and yours. You wanted me, like you wanted all of us, your older students, to remain in surrender and obedience to you, and to serve "our work"—your life project. So I can understand why, when I became a strong, independent leader, you felt, "Fantastic—I have another strong person surrendered to me and serving our work!" While for me, finally becoming independent after twenty-something years with you required that I create some distance from you. I was actually de-surrendering to you, if you want, as part of my individuation process. Therefore, your call to me to go back to the U.S. and be close to you again felt like you were trying to undermine that process, which made me mistrust your motives and judgment and therefore say, "Forget it, you're wrong and I'm going to do what's right," which to me meant the end of our teacher-student contract.

ANDREW: I see. That makes sense to me. You're saying that you didn't really want to leave, but because of my responses to you, you felt that you had no choice. So had I been more trusting of the process and less controlling, had I stopped holding everything on such a tight leash and allowed you and many of my other older students to go in the directions you needed to go, maybe there would have been an organic evolution of the whole body.

AMIR: I don't know. Maybe there would have been a development of the whole body and maybe it would have collapsed. Maybe a breakup was unavoidable. Not only because of how you mishandled our need for individuation, but because there is an inherent clash between surrender to the guru and autonomy, and the two may be incompatible with each other.

ANDREW: I don't see why, if the need for individuation is understood, recognized and allowed, if not encouraged, there would have to be such a clash. To put it another way, it's possible that parents would be so evolved, so sophisticated, so integrally developed, that a child wouldn't have to rebel against them in order to individuate. That happens sometimes. If everything is done right, and the developmental context is very sophisticated, then individuation can happen without the need for rebellion. And if it can happen in a parent-child relationship, it must also be possible in the Guru-disciple relationship.

Surrender or submission to a living teacher, although looked down upon by our current culture as synonymous with weakness of mind and character, has been recognized in many traditions and paths as an essential pillar of the spiritual journey. One of the main reasons for this is that it plays an essential role in the student's transcending their ego-personality or self-protection and allowing a deeper self to emerge. In the words of Ronald Jue, past president of the Association of Transpersonal Psychology, "Within a transpersonal perspective, one can reach a point of surrender in which a deeper sense of self emerges, one that goes beyond the boundaries of ego and does not rest upon one's self-identity or personality." For the very same reason, surrender is also the ultimate challenge for the student, as expressed by Indologist Georg Feuerstein in his book *Holy Madness: The Shock Tactics and Radical Teachings of Crazy-Wise Adepts, Holy Fools and Rascal Gurus*:

> *In authentic spiritual discipleship, submission is immediate and concrete. The disciple's surrender is demanded and seen by the teacher. Good intentions and verbal declarations do not suffice. The guru fully expects precisely the kind of actions that the abstract God of popular devotion benignly overlooks. The ordinary individual shudders at the prospect of delivering himself or herself so completely to the mercy of another person. The common fear of submission to another being springs from the firsthand experience of egoic existence: The ego-personality is experienced as a locus of power. In its paranoid need to assert and protect itself, the ego-personality looks constantly for ways to remain in control of events.*

Autonomy, by which I would include the concepts of independence, individuation, self-authority, self-actualization and self-responsibility, is highly revered in our modern-postmodern culture and an achievement we expect of any genuine process of spiritual growth and maturation. In the context of a teacher-student relationship, it is to develop while the student is in close relationship with a person they revere, admire and consider superior to them in some of the most important ways. In the words of spiritual teacher Omraam Mikhaël Aïvanhov, from his book *What Is a Spiritual Master?*:

> *Everybody has his own path, his mission, and even if you take your Master as a model, you must always develop in the way that suits your own nature. You have to sing the part which has been given to you, aware of the notes, the beat and the rhythm; you have to sing it with your own voice which is certainly not that of your Master,*

but that is not important. The one really important thing is to sing your part perfectly.

But *can* the student "sing their part perfectly," as Aïvanhov puts it, in the context of surrender to a teacher? Since surrender to a teacher seems to inherently involve at least some abdication of self-authority and responsibility, while autonomy means little if not full self-authority and responsibility, they appear to be incompatible. The internal contradiction and confusion that this paradox causes, is evident in the following words of Buddhist teacher and author Stephen Batchelor (in an issue of *Insight Newsletter*):

The extent to which one relies on one's own clarity of mind, or to what extent does one relinquish that, at least temporarily, to rely upon the clarity of mind of another person—that's the tension. In my own experience, I have oscillated back and forth between these two... And that is central to my understanding of Buddhist tradition: part of the practice is to rely upon others, yes, but not if that requires a denial of one's own autonomy.

If, or as long as, surrender and autonomy remain in conflict with each other, autonomy may be achievable only upon breakup of the teacher-student relationship, as evident in Andrew's stories of his breakup with his teacher and with me. This possibility was supported by the story told by Integral thinker, author and coach Terry Patten in my interview with him:

TERRY PATTEN

TERRY: I was with Adi Da for fifteen years, starting in the very early days of his teaching in Los Angeles and Northern California. The awakening, transmission, brilliance, the sweetness of love-bliss that I experienced with him were off the chart. So was the richness of the new Dharma that he brought through, and the art and poetry. He was thoroughly authentic in the richest possible way. At the same time, the structure of this relationship was totally, intensely hierarchical. He was the guru. We were the devotees. Zero mutuality. The work ended up always being about the miracle of Him, capitalized.

I'm not interested in criticizing him because the first, second or third things I want to say about him have to do with gratitude and praise. It was a tremendous gift to spend such an intense transformational time with him. In some sense, all the traditional devotional language that "I'm just a reflection of what my guru gave me" has a truth to it. Although I went through years of processing anger and confusion, I circled back to being devotionally grateful to him and I will forever be grateful for everything I received through that relationship, which remains profoundly transformative.

And it's also true, in a sense, that he failed me. He failed to trust and honor the spiritual process that he initiated in me. I had to stand up and say "no" to him, and eventually I had to leave the ashram altogether. After I left I had a profound awakening. The same happened with Saniel Bonder [Chapter 9]. In our experience, it was as if a secret teaching was revealed only in the process of leaving the teaching. It was as if it was printed on the inside of the wrapper, made visible only in the process of us liberating ourselves from it.

AMIR: It sounds like you're holding two completely different perspectives on your relationship with him.

TERRY: Yes, it's pretty complex, and I'm still working it out. I have a huge body of experience that makes no sense except in the mode of grateful surrendered adoration of my guru. And I have another huge body of experience that makes no sense except when, having summoned up my autonomous self-discernment and self-responsibility, I am saying no and giving the finger to the many ways I was violated and victimized by the unhealthy dynamics. I can't be in the state that can access the first body of experience and the state that can access the other body of experience at the same time. Those states are incompatible; they are mutually exclusive. So I've been forced to live with the fact that I will never be able to contain the totality of the experience I lived in this body, because of my encounter with Adi

Da. It's a profound and paradoxical teaching. For that, I'm eternally grateful.

I will end this chapter with the words of philosopher Joachim Wach from his article "Master and Disciple: Two Religio-Sociological Studies," in which he suggests that autonomy becomes possible only if and when the student departs from the teacher:

> *The most sacred moment in the relation of the master to his disciple comes when the master finally turns the disciple back to himself; it reveals the significance of the master for his disciple; it is the moment in which the relationship is most intimate. Yet, at the same time, it is that moment in which the master appears most remote: above the relationship of master and disciple is written the word "farewell." It is the specific tragedy of the master's life that he is destined to direct everything toward this parting. Instead of completely drawing to himself, he must completely thrust away; instead of moving from distance to the intimate unity, he must move in the opposite direction.*
>
> *Therefore, the master can only love his disciple with a tinge of sadness. The disciple does not understand the master, though the master means everything to him; he loses himself in the greatness of the master and seeks to comprehend him existentially. His highest goal is to be most intimately related to this master. So "he follows after him," until the hour of decision comes, which always must be the hour of parting; then the disciple despairs either of the master or of himself. He must choose either himself and take leave of the master, who was dearer to him than all things, or he must deny himself, continuing to love the master, and so destroy completely the master's labor.*

CHAPTER 13
WHOSE UNDERSTANDING IS IT ANYWAY?

When a person who is intensely alive also has great originality of mind, the impact on those who work with him is a blend in which intellectual substance and spell of personality are difficult to disentangle. It has been said that students of Wittgenstein are unable to distinguish between what they gained from him philosophically and what the impress of his compelling personality made them feel they had gained... The intensity of his inner life and the compelling force of his own values communicated themselves to others and made demands for adjustment to him.

—ALICE AMBROSE AND MORRIS LAZEROWITZ, *LUDWIG WITTGENSTEIN: PHILOSOPHY AND LANGUAGE*

[Wittgenstein] thought that his influence as a teacher was, on the whole, harmful to the development of independent minds in his disciples. I am afraid that he was right. And I believed that I can partly understand why it should be so. Because of the depth and originality of his thinking, it is very difficult to understand Wittgenstein's ideas and even more difficult to incorporate them into one's own thinking. At the same time the magic of his personality and style was most inviting and persuasive. To learn from Wittgenstein without coming to adopt his forms of expression and catchwords and even to imitate his tone of voice, his mien and gestures

*was almost impossible. The danger was that the thoughts should deterio-
rate into a jargon. The teaching of great men often has the simplicity and
naturalness which makes the difficult appear easy to grasp. Their disciples
usually become, therefore, insignificant epigones.*

—GEORG HENRIK VON WRIGHT, QUOTED IN *LUDWIG
WITTGENSTEIN: A MEMOIR BY NORMAN MALCOLM*

STEVE BRETT AND MARY ADAMS

Steve Brett and Mary Adams were formerly close students of
Andrew Cohen for over two decades. Presently, Steve is completing
his M.A. in South Asian studies, Mary is writing a book on women's
leadership, and they host intercultural dialogues and give talks in
London and India. I interviewed them together for a few hours at
their London apartment. Out of that interview, I selected a section
in which Steve spoke about his meeting with Andrew, and the three
of us explored the question of the student's spiritual-philosophical
understanding.

AMIR: Steve, why don't we start with your meeting with Andrew?
Did you have any inkling of what was going to happen before you
met him?

STEVE: To be honest, I didn't really expect much when I met him.
He was somebody I had heard about from a close friend so I was
curious, and I was always interested in meeting genuine teachers
because I was a real seeker. I think that Andrew probably had some
idea of my background, as someone involved in Buddhist meditation who had been to India for a long time. Anyway, I went to see
him in the small cottage he was staying in in England at the time,
and we had a long conversation up in his room. He asked me a lot of
questions about my spiritual life and so forth. Andrew seemed like
a very unassuming person and I was struck by how natural and at
ease he was. Other than that, there wasn't really anything unusual
about him.

So we were in the midst of this conversation and he was asking me about my life, and suddenly my mind completely stopped. For no apparent reason, it literally stopped in the middle of this discussion. Now, I'd had a lot of spiritual experiences before, but this had never happened to me. Andrew was completely tuned in to what was going on. He said to me, "What's going on right now?" And I replied, "My mind just stopped." It's hard to describe, but all sense of separation disappeared in that moment. There was this immediate realization of all existence being One. I mean, it was a very profound experience, but I didn't have any words for it. So I told Andrew that my mind had stopped. And all he said was, "Now we are really communicating." Then he added, "You have jumped in the river and now you have to decide if you want this. But you might not have any choice." My experience was that we were sitting in this space of Oneness together. Only he was totally relaxed, completely unfazed by it, while I was in a state of shock, literally shaking all over. I mean, this sense of the unity of existence was totally overwhelming.

AMIR: Could you communicate while in that space?

STEVE: Oh yes, I was talking to Andrew while all this was happening, describing what was going on, and he was asking me about it. It was a very unusual event. I had never experienced anything like it. And also what made it so unusual was that we were in it together, and that was very clear to me.

Anyway, after a few minutes, my mind suddenly came back very fast and started throwing up all these questions and trying to figure out what had just happened. This went on for a while, and then we went downstairs and had dinner together with others who were staying in the house, but I was in a completely altered state. I mean, I was aware of all that was going on, but I was somewhere else. The experience seemed to have taken over my whole being.

AMIR: Did you feel that this was what you were looking for?

STEVE: Well, the thing is that it was too much for me at the time to reflect on because it was so overwhelming. I knew it was everything in some way, but I couldn't step back and reflect on it. So what happened was that the next day I went back to London and went to work—I was working as a therapist at the time. But then this sense of an infinite expansion would start happening spontaneously out of the blue. Like when I was sitting on a bus going to work, it would completely overwhelm me and I would find myself in a profound state of meditation. Or I would be walking down the street and suddenly be over-taken taken by this thing. At times it was very powerful—one time it happened when I was lying on my bed and I felt pinned to the spot by this utterly ecstatic force and couldn't move. It was like the source of the universe itself literally pouring through me.

So I started to call up Andrew and tell him what was going on, and I realized that I was actually describing the experience I had been looking for for years and now it was coming directly from me. It was not coming from my mind at all and I was amazed that I could actually verbalize it. Whenever I spoke to him about it, the experience would become amplified, and it was clear to me that he was the source of it.

AMIR: How is it possible, that it came directly from you and still Andrew was the source of it?

STEVE: Well, for me, because I had this experience when I met him, I could never see him as a person separate from myself. I mean, the experience of non-separation was completely related to him and this was the foundation of our relationship. Of course, that non-separation was also with other people, but with Andrew it was of a different nature, simply because he was the source of it.

AMIR: So you never had to actually accept him as your teacher, you just slipped into it.

STEVE: Actually, another thing happened at that time which was very significant, and this was quite strange because it also happened completely spontaneously. I was with Andrew in his house, and I said to him quite suddenly, "I want to be with you for the rest of my life." It was a statement that came totally out of nowhere. I hadn't planned to say that. I mean, I would have never even conceived of such a thing. But it was an absolute declaration that I felt I had to say at that particular moment. I remember that Andrew was very moved by that.

AMIR: It's interesting that your declaration wasn't "I want to give my life to *this*," but it had to do with wanting to be with *him*.

STEVE: Well, again, because Andrew was the source of what had happened, to me they were one and the same thing. I know it came from a very deep place in myself, beyond thought. I think it was a response from my soul to what I had received and to the person I had received it from. But I didn't really conceptualize it.

AMIR: It is a powerful declaration of devotion and surrender; did you feel any fear or doubt related to it?

STEVE: Oh, definitely. When we moved to America and I had lived in Andrew's house for a couple of weeks, I remember waking up in the middle of the night terrified, in a cold sweat, because I knew I had left my own life behind. This terror would just happen and I couldn't do anything about it, and then it would pass. And I think it was directly related to the declaration I had made to Andrew.

AMIR: I'd like to ask you something, Steve, that comes from my memory of you at the time, because I got to know you a few months after you met Andrew. I remember being very impressed by the depth of your insight and understanding, and your ability to express it with clarity and precision. Do you also see that depth and clarity as coming from him—as being a result of being in his aura, so to speak?

STEVE: The experience I had when I met Andrew, although initiated by Andrew, was very much my own. Still, such an experience has enormous implications, that take many years to come to terms with. You know, you're just a regular person with your strengths and weaknesses, and suddenly you have this earth-shattering experience, that has nothing to do with where you are at as a human being. So coming to terms with it requires a process of maturation and integration, of closing the gap between what you realized and where you're at. This process can, but doesn't necessarily have to do with being within the aura of the teacher.

MARY: Honestly, Steve, I think that during that time you were able to articulate and demonstrate an understanding that was not exactly where you were actually at. You weren't faking it—it was because your spiritual awakening was sustained through the relationship with Andrew. It's almost inevitable that during the period one is in the close proximity of a teacher like Andrew, that one's level of consciousness remains elevated through their contact with that teacher. It happens naturally but it's not necessarily reflective of where one is really at in terms of depth, spiritual maturity or even clarity.

AMIR: You have to take into consideration, Mary, that in general it's very difficult and maybe impossible to separate the experience from the interpretation you give it; so if the teacher leads the way, then your experience is interpreted through the conceptual framework and language that the teacher provides.

MARY: I agree, and I think this is one of the core dilemmas or challenges of that relationship. In the spiritual experience, you are awakening to something that is in you, that is your essential nature; but then what you discover has to be lived, explored, understood and expanded, and this takes a long process. During that process, if you're in the proximity of the teacher—absorbing the transmission of their teachings and in an engaged relationship with them—it can be very hard for you to know what's "yours" and what isn't. And as a student, it's actually important that you know that, despite the experience of spiritual awakening, "This is not my knowledge yet, it's what I'm absorbing from my teacher," and be aware of the gap that is still there.

AMIR: Both of you had a long history of spiritual seeking *before* you met Andrew—you, Mary, in Advaita Vedanta, and you in Buddhism, Steve. So how was it for you to make the shift to the concepts and language of Andrew's teachings of Evolutionary Enlightenment?

MARY: As you know, Andrew was a student of Poonjaji, who was a disciple of the legendary Sri Ramana Maharshi, and initially Andrew's teachings were fairly classical Advaita teachings of non-duality—of awakening to one's true nature as One. But the expression of this, in a contemporary Western form, from someone almost my own age—I was thirty-three at the time—had a powerful immediacy. Also, what attracted me to Andrew most was that, almost from the beginning, he stressed the importance of the relationship between spiritual realization and our actions in time and space. His emphasis was not on the attainment of powerful spiritual experiences as an end in themselves, but on the potential and implications of these for living an enlightened life; especially the potential for an enlightened collective.

Having spent years engaged in an inwardly focused spiritual enquiry, based on solitary practice, removed from the world, Andrew's message seemed, to me, the true meaning of the nondual teachings. The shift, that occurred about ten years later, to Evolutionary Enlightenment, according to which the entire cosmos, including one's consciousness, is evolving in perpetuity, made deep sense to me. This seemed a natural progression in the teachings themselves; and as an interpretation, or iteration of nonduality seemed to provide a perfect answer as to why we are all here, and what is the relationship between the One and the many.

AMIR: In most teacher-student relationships, the teacher and the teaching are perceived as inseparable from the experience of the absolute. In other words, there is an assumption of unity between the experience of the absolute and the specific interpretation provided by the teacher, which makes it nearly impossible for the student to step out of that framework and examine it more objectively.

STEVE: I don't see it as a problem. It seems to me that it's just part of that particular relationship and hopefully it's only a phase. It may be quite a long phase, but the process is very long anyway. What I mean is that in order to find your own independence you have to first become deeply engaged with a teacher. Then you're in a process and you can't objectify the process you're in, you literally can't. Surrender requires a kind of letting go of that kind of objectivity.

AMIR: Steve, when you say that it's impossible to objectify, you're not saying that it's impossible to think for yourself and discriminate, are you?

STEVE: To me, there has to be a trust in the process. It doesn't mean you become an idiot, but there's something in the relationship itself that calls for this kind of surrender. I think this is what it's supposed to be about—the kind of surrender where there's deep trust and love between the student and the teacher, so deep that the student is able to fully let go. This kind of experience is essential, at least initially.

AMIR: Are you suggesting that in the early stage of the relationship it's better to put aside the question of autonomy and discrimination, so that you can experience, at least for a period of time, the benefits of trust and surrender?

STEVE: Well, I think that you have to go through a phase where you wholeheartedly adopt their way and deeply absorb what they give you. Then, later in the process, there may be lessons, sometimes painful ones, that will make you independent of the teacher.

MARY: Andrew possessed an original mind, as well as an intense personality. The sheer strength of his conviction, along with an incisive clarity and subtlety of communication, created a powerful transmission that literally resonated within us, his students. His words bypassed our minds yet registered with a profound intellectual clarity. This unmitigated experience of a higher order of knowledge is what made his teachings so exhilarating.

I think it's true that this kind of "transmitted" wisdom was not *ours* as such; it was not integrated. But in time, I believe, we grew into it. This was largely due to the intensive enquiry we engaged in ongoingly, both alone and together, against a backdrop of equally intensive spiritual practice. Also, Andrew constantly tested our understanding and our spiritual maturity, by creating austere, often harsh conditions. He was quick to observe movements of ego—impulses in the human psyche towards self-aggrandizement, abuse of power, arrogance, doubt, weakness in the face of fear, etcetera—and he was swift to respond to these. The degree to which we were independent in our own spiritual grounding, and had truly integrated the principles and insights afforded by his teachings, was transparent both to ourselves and to those around us. Our lives thus became potential vehicles for spiritual maturation and development.

AMIR: Steve spoke about wholeheartedly absorbing what the teacher gives you, does that include also the teacher's preferences in music, movies, food, clothing, etc.? Could you make a distinction between the spiritual transmission you received from Andrew and what was just an arbitrary aspect of his personality?

MARY: There was, from fairly early on, a commingling of the spiritual and philosophical substantiveness of Andrew's realization with his personal characteristics—biases, preferences and attitudes. He himself did not make a distinction between these, regarding his personal predilections as expressions of a higher order of consciousness. So, within the context of complete surrender to the Guru, as we previously discussed, there was also a tendency in those of us, who were Andrew's closest students, to absorb his personal attributes— both positive and negative. Initially, this was not overt but, gradually, over time, Andrew's habits of impeccably dressing, maintaining a rigorous physical workout routine, eating specific foods and always pushing one's own limits, became identified in our minds as expressions of a higher consciousness—something we consciously, and unconsciously, emulated.

There were elements to this with regard to developing self-discipline, such as working out regularly, eating healthy food, caring for one's appearance and environment, that made sense to me, and I appreciated the aesthetics involved. But from early on, I also found myself struggling at times with some of the areas where Andrew expected us to adopt his views. Examples of this were his taste in films, his political attitudes, views on gender and parenting, and later, his increasingly harsh or dismissive ways of responding to people. Some of this jarred with my own sensibilities, and I found myself, on occasion, deeply at odds with Andrew. However, as he became increasingly confident as a teacher, he also became increasingly authoritarian. I then tended to submerge my differences—either genuinely submitting to what I assumed was a higher perspective or, at times, acquiescing out of a fear of being rebuked, or alienated. This resulted in a growing self-doubt and worse—burying my own conscience.

Throughout my time with Andrew, however, I maintained a deep trust in him, as my teacher, at a *fundamental* level, and a conviction in the spiritual truths he was able to transmit. This had very mixed consequences.

AMIR: Can you say a bit more about the mixed consequences?

MARY: This is a huge and controversial question, as Andrew's student body not only incorporated multiple variations of experience—from the sublime to the horrific—but we also hold multiple interpretations of our experience, including how we judge the entirety of our history. It's a human event still in process.

Speaking for myself, very briefly, my trust in Andrew as my teacher, at a fundamental level, allowed me to *let go*. Through this relationship, I was able to go beyond the boundaries of what I thought I knew, who I thought I was, and the way I understood the world or reality to be. This opened up experiences and insight beyond anything I had previously imagined—a depth of being, and appreciation of the multi-dimensionality of life and existence, that is endless. This occurred through a meeting with Andrew, where I experienced an intimacy of Self in which there was literally no "other." This profound experience, rather than the man himself, imbued me with a fundamental trust in life.

However, because I, and many of us, with Andrew's encouragement, grew to regard the *man* as inseparable from that experience of trust, I gave up much of my discriminatory power. As a result, I did not question Andrew or things that slowly crept into our culture and became normal—actions and attitudes that were clearly wrong and, in many cases, destructive.

So, my trust in Andrew and what I was called to within myself, which is a higher potential for human beings, on one hand, gave me the strength and commitment to go through genuine spiritual ordeals and grow. And this, similar with others, created a foundation for some extraordinary breakthroughs and developments in collective higher consciousness. The other side to this relationship with Andrew, as mentioned, is that through the denial of personal conscience, compliance with structures that became increasingly cultish, resulted in indefensible suffering for many.

From the beginning of my own spiritual seeking at the age of sixteen until I met Andrew Cohen, a dozen years later, my search was motivated by the disturbing realization, that my connection with reality was mediated, distorted and limited by conceptual filters. Having realized that, I became determined to know reality directly, without the distorting and limiting effect of any filters. For this very reason, during the time I practiced Zen with a teacher in Japan I once responded to his offer to teach me the basics of Buddhist philosophy by explaining to him that my purpose was to remove, through practice, the filters I had, not to replace them with Buddhist ones.

Then, as a result of my meeting Andrew and the insights and revelations that followed, I stopped being a seeker and became a finder: I knew the taste of unitive consciousness and could attest, from firsthand experience, to the ever-presence of the ultimate reality. The thing is, I was aware that when I did that, I used the same concepts, even the same words, that Andrew did. Love, for example, which previously was completely absent from my "spiritual jargon," suddenly became a central concept—how did that happen? When I looked into my experience of the ultimate reality it was empty of words, concepts, images or feelings, but when I spoke about it, I found no other words, concepts, images and feelings but those I somehow acquired from Andrew. Did I really know? Was my understanding my own or was it Andrew's? This question haunted me until, one day, I decided that, in light of all the unimaginable blessings I was receiving through my connection with Andrew, this question was only an expression of pride and ego, and I dropped it altogether. The tension I had experienced around that question was relieved, but looking at that decision now, from a thirty-year distance, I recognize that in that decision I sacrificed, at least temporarily, my critical thinking.

As Steve's and Mary's stories and my own story demonstrate, and as anyone who spent time with a charismatic teacher or thinker knows, after spending some time with a master it becomes quite difficult to separate one's own understanding from theirs. This is true not only for spiritual teachers and their students—the quotes at the beginning of this chapter, from two students of the renowned philosopher Ludwig Wittgenstein, attest to the powerful influence he had on them—and to their ensuing confusion about their own understanding. Apparently, this dynamic can occur in any hierarchical relationship, and in the context of a teacher-student relationship, it begs the question: Can the student be an independent experiencer and interpreter of their experience while in relationship with a teacher?

EPILOGUE

When I started seeking spiritually, at the age of sixteen, spiritual-existential questions were the source and core of my seeking. *Who am I? What is all this? What is life for?* I felt that, as long as I didn't know the answers to these basic questions, I was simply wasting my life. I desperately had to find the answers.

Then, at the age of twenty-nine, I underwent an event of unitive consciousness, and all my questions dissolved in a realization of a different order. In an instant, from a spiritual seeker I became a finder. I saw that those questions were merely pale reflections of the great mystery of Everything. The questions disappeared in that realization.

Once the smoke cleared, however, I found that new and just as powerful and meaningful questions, which sprang out of the realization of unitive consciousness, took the place of the old ones. These questions, I realized, were not to be resolved but to be lived; and answers were not to bring an end to questioning, but to allow for old questions to be replaced with new and fresh ones.

Living in a state of questioning, searching and exploring became for me an end, rather than a means to an end; and I've been living in that state to this very day.

It is not surprising, therefore, that my exploration into the spiritual teacher-student relationship leads to the conclusion, that paradoxes and dilemmas are inherent to this relationship and are not to be "solved," but rather to be lived as openly, dynamically and unre-servedly as possible. In fact, paradoxes and dilemmas are the beating heart of the spiritual teacher-student relationship; and as long as they are vibrantly and dynamically alive, so is the relationship.

AFTERWORD

KEN WILBER

The theme of this important volume is "spiritual transmission"—the transmission of a special spiritual awareness from a teacher to a student—which is actually an issue that affects most forms of spiritual training. But its spiritual forms are especially associated with teachers known as "gurus" and with the entire path of Guru Yoga. And that overall path is what I'm going to focus on, because the whole topic of there being a guru or spiritual master is truly one of the most pressing and profound issues of our time.

The underlying idea of Guru Yoga is the notion that, in order to receive the guru's spiritual "transmission," you must surrender to the guru; you must voluntarily turn your life—or large portions of it—over to somebody else, somebody who allegedly knows more than you do in this area, and you choose to submit yourself to that person in order to receive that learning. At its base is the question of selfsovereignty and self-autonomy itself: when is it appropriate to voluntarily surrender one's own autonomy and turn it over to somebody else, and occasionally in quite far-reaching and extensive ways?

Guru Yoga, in its developed forms, is several thousand years old. It appears wherever there is a major cultural/spiritual context that maintains that the typical human state is "ignorant," "fallen" or "illusory," and that this condition can be reversed with a state said to be "enlightened" or "awakened." To spell that out a bit, the belief is that human beings are born into an alienated, or dualistic and fragmented world that is inherently one of suffering and massive ignorance.

In this fallen world, humans are identified with a very narrow, broken and partial self-identity (often called the "ego"), which is said to be a major delusion, a false consciousness that drives suffering, pain and almost endless torment. But, the major spiritual traditions further claim, humans have the capacity to awaken from this fractured dream and discover not only their own True Self or real Nature, they can also discover the glorious Ground of All Being itself—or pure Spirit. And what's more, their True Self is said to be absolutely one with this infinite Spirit—what the Sufis call the "Supreme Identity." This extraordinary transformation—from fractured ego-self to divine spiritual Self—is variously known around the world as Enlightenment, Awakening, Metamorphosis, Fana, Satori, Realization, Moksha, the Great Liberation—in short, "Waking Up."

The way that the Great Traditions pictured this transformation was based on what was called the "Two Truths" doctrine—namely, there are two basic truths, relative and absolute truth or ultimate Truth. Relative truth has to do with the manifest, finite world: human beings need food to survive; the sun rises in the east and sets in the west; water can exist in three states, as ice or water or steam; and so on. Those are all relative truths, and the Great Traditions don't deny any of those a relative reality. But there is also ultimate Truth which maintains things like, "Water and ice and humans themselves are all direct manifestations of ultimate Spirit (or a Ground of All Being)." So the Great Traditions maintain that their specific Paths of Liberation (including Guru Yoga), help an individual transform from being lost in relative truth to being awakened to ultimate Truth.

In these various traditions (East and West), once a person has discovered their own True Self, they can in turn act as catalysts of this discovery for other people. Such a realized individual, in other words, can become a guru. The stated aim of a guru is to use various techniques (including direct transmission) in order to help their students awaken to ultimate Truth. To understand what that originally meant and what it still tends to mean, it's important to remember that most of these traditions are at least 2,000 years old. At that time, science had not yet been discovered; humans didn't yet understand that the earth circled the sun; that evolution had a hand in creating all living creatures; knew nothing of brain chemistry and neurotransmitters and their profound role in altering awareness; slavery was still perfectly acceptable and often encouraged; women in general were second-class citizens, if that; life expectancy was around thirty years; poverty rate worldwide was over ninety-five percent.

But all of that ignorance was considered completely secondary to a much deeper and infinitely more profound ignorance: namely, ignorance of the primordial Ground of All Being—ignorance not of relative truth, but of ultimate Truth. No matter how correctly—or incorrectly—one understood various aspects of the relative, manifest universe, all of that paled in comparison to the fact that the entire universe itself was nothing but a manifestation of an ultimate Spirit, an ultimate Ground of Being, and if one was not directly aware of that infinite Ground and ultimate Truth, then one was hopelessly lost, no matter how much relative knowledge one might have.

And thus, in order to reverse this state of profound ignorance, a person needed to take up one of the authentic Paths of Liberation offered by the various Great Traditions—and a primary version of these paths was that of Guru Yoga. What all of the Paths of Liberation had in common was the practice of various exercises that decommissioned the ordinary state of egoic consciousness and its basic mental operations, and replaced them with a direct realization of the Supreme Identity and ultimate Truth in one's own case. The version of this "decommissioning process" that original Guru Yoga took included having the student consistently take up an attitude of, "Everything I think and do is wrong, and everything the guru thinks and does is right." That was either part of the actual instructions of the particular path, or it was the attitude that almost every student eventually ended up taking in the course of their training.

After all, the guru is God-realized; and clearly, God doesn't make mistakes. This is, in effect, the basis for the voluntary surrendering of self-autonomy in order to transcend the ego and discover one's own True Self. And in some pragmatic cases, this practice works exactly as it is supposed to. Since most human beings are almost totally identified with their ego and largely ignorant of their True Self, by consistently undercutting the ego with that total self-deprecation, the ego could indeed be largely decommissioned, allowing the Self to more easily shine through. In these positive cases, the student goes from being totally identified with the ego—with all its misery and suffering—and starts to resonate with the True Self of the guru. The student then uses that resonance to start to recognize their own True Self, and with further practice, to shift their identity profoundly from their typical ego to that Supreme Identity, that ultimate Truth per se.

That ultimate Truth is certainly the basic core claim of virtually all of the world's Great Wisdom Traditions, and no matter how often that ultimate Truth was surrounded by relative truths that were in fact misconceptions, that core Truth remains the central offering of the Great Wisdom Traditions. That ultimate realization is certainly the core of the truth that is claimed by Guru Yoga and therefore the point in fairly and effectively critiquing Guru Yoga—attempting to understand both its strengths and its weaknesses—is to do so while also accepting the fundamental existence and reality of these basic satori-like realizations. That is to say, that any effective, fair and accurate critique of Guru Yoga will accept the existence of the Two Truths doctrine. If we reject an ultimate Truth altogether (one that can be experientially realized with Enlightenment or Awakening), then there is nothing whatsoever that recommends Guru Yoga—it degenerates entirely into nothing but a type of indentured servitude. It takes no real thinking at all to simply reject any guru principle on the grounds that it severely violates individual autonomy. Yet to point out the obvious, that's exactly what it's supposed to do (at least temporarily). But the real point is that when (as almost every critic invariably does), we make the rational ego into ultimate Truth, then anything that violates the ego and its absolute sovereignty is taken to be demonic or delusional—and that certainly includes Guru Yoga (and the rest of the Paths of Liberation). Merely reacting to Guru Yoga as a vicious "autonomy violation" is not much more than a platitude, and mindlessly reflects the typical modern notion that an independent and autonomous ego is the highest reality known to humankind, whereas, according to virtually all of the Great Traditions, it's simply the height of illusion.

So the only serious question in a genuine critique of Guru Yoga becomes: How adequate, how authentic, how effective is Guru Yoga when it comes to transmitting ultimate Truth? How good is Guru Yoga at helping individuals discover their own True Self and Supreme Identity, at realizing a genuine Enlightenment and true Awakening? What we discover, I believe, is that during the time that Guru Yoga was originally created (some two to three thousand years ago), the social and cultural conditions were such that it was largely an authentic and quite effective version of the Paths of Liberation. But as humanity moved into the modern and postmodern era, with its increasing sociocultural evolution, the relative truths that surrounded Guru Yoga became less and less acceptable, so that finally, the core of ultimate Truth that it contained was surrounded by so many relative truths that were increasingly misguided, false and damaging, that Guru Yoga indeed became reduced to almost nothing more than a useless and damaging violation of individual autonomy. Authentic satori was rarely achieved, and in its place were often anxiety, depression and a badly broken relative self.

However, I will also suggest that if the relative truths surrounding Guru Yoga are significantly readjusted (while keeping its core of a valid Enlightenment and ultimate Unity Realization), then Guru Yoga can indeed return to being a very viable—and especially effective—form of spiritual training and genuine Awakening.

The core of the problem, I believe, centers around the "totalistic" nature of the authority that many versions of Guru Yoga place in the person of the guru—namely the central stance of *infallibility*. A central reason that a student is willing to submit to the guru is indeed the idea that the guru can be fully trusted in this area—that the guru is infallible—and whether that claim is explicitly made by the Path itself, which it often is, or whether it is simply assumed by the student, which it virtually always is, the core issue remains the surrendering of self-autonomy by the student and the assumption of infallibility given to the guru.

The major foundation of this notion of infallibility was indeed the Two Truths: The guru might not know every little relative truth in the world that there is to know, but the guru does know ultimate Truth. This means that the guru's ignorance of relative truth simply doesn't ultimately matter, because the relative realm doesn't really matter.

This belief was easy to maintain, especially given the way in which a genuine satori seemed to clarify and fully handle all of the items in the relative realm. To enter nirvana was to touch a ground of Reality so real and so profound, it thoroughly dominated anything the relative world and its relative truths could say or do—and it certainly demonstrated that everything in the relative realm (known as "samsara") was truly illusory and unreal. It's important to realize that nirvana was not just a theological notion, nor a metaphysical idea, nor a mere philosophical belief. It was a direct, immediate, unmistakable experience, delivered directly to consciousness itself and fully reproducible in others. Nirvana could even overcome—in a very direct and provable fashion—the most intense pain known to humans. This wasn't just an exaggerated or boastful claim, it was literally quite true: enter the state of nirvana, a state of cessation that was totally painless, formless, empty—and in that state one was free of pain and suffering and ego altogether. We saw screaming, shocking examples of this purely formless painless state—and its incredible reality—during the Vietnam War, when monks protesting the war sat in meditation posture, entered the formless painless state—entered "nirvana"—and had their bodies doused in gasoline and then set on fire; right there on live TV, in front of millions, they burned to the ground in ashes, and not one of them even flinched once. This very real nirvana state is in part behind many of the experiences found in near-death experiences, spontaneous spiritual peak experiences, and specific states of meditation, which is what makes so many of them feel so undeniably real.

The question is not therefore, as I've said, whether nirvana is real or not. Rather, the significant question, especially when it comes to Guru Yoga, is exactly what types of truth does a satori or Waking-Up experience convey in the first place? What does nirvana *actually tell you*? After all, the many cultures that had full access to Waking-Up experiences—and a very large majority of the traditional great civilizations certainly did—still knew nothing about atoms, molecules or cells; knew nothing about the functioning of television or radio or computers; didn't know the earth circled the sun or even that it wasn't flat; had no idea that women could be equal citizens or that slavery was immoral.

Those facts—namely, that the reality of nirvana seems to be an ultimate Truth—has remained true up to and including the Vietnam War period, but many of the specific relative truths of earlier times have not stood up well at all, which means that the safest *generalization* about the Two Truths is that a Waking-Up experience will give you ample knowledge about ultimate Truth, but almost no knowledge about relative truth at all.

So whereas today's typical criticism about Guru Yoga is that it dominates an individual's ego and takes away their autonomy, a more cogent criticism would be that the guru's authority is limited to those areas dealing only with ultimate Truth—since ultimate Truth is the only truth that satori guarantees. Satori can tell us that we are perfectly One with that tree; but it cannot tell us a thing about the most elementary particles of that tree, including the fact that the tree itself is made of cells and molecules and atoms and quarks. Ultimate Truth is limited strictly to items having to do with the nature and qualities of ultimate Reality itself, and indeed the various Paths of Liberation are replete with treatises on just that ultimate Nature and its various characteristics. But when it comes to qualities and factors that pertain to relative truth and to a relative finite human being per se, gurus (and their satoris) are extremely fallible. In terms of pure significance, ultimate Truth is infinitely beyond any relative truth. But when it comes to the sheer number of truths, relative truth is overwhelming—and, besides, when it comes to the ultimate One, there is only, so to speak, One of those to know, compared to trillions upon trillions of relative truths.

Furthermore, the nondual revolution that would soon sweep the spiritual world—beginning with Nagarjuna's astonishing treatises on *shunyata*—would profoundly change the understanding of the very relation between nirvana and samsara. According to Nagarjuna, nirvana is still a very real state, but it is not quite truly ultimate. In its original version, nirvana is completely split and divorced from samsara, and the aim of Realization is to totally get off (the "wheel" of) samsara and embrace only nirvana. It was, in other words, a deeply dualistic notion, with the universe split right down the middle into half real and half illusory. Nagarjuna points out that, although the nirvana state is indeed real, there is a yet deeper and even more real state, which he called "shunyata," which literally means "Emptiness," but in a special sense: it doesn't directly mean formless or nothingness. It means radically *unqualifiable*, totally beyond any characterization whatsoever; and it is radically beyond any characterization at all because Emptiness is the Reality that equally contains all of them. Thus, being radically all-inclusive, Emptiness underlies and embraces both nirvana and samsara. That is, nirvana and samsara are two different aspects of the same underlying Wholeness—a Wholeness Nagarjuna called "Nonduality," since nirvana and samsara were "non-dual" or "not-two" or ultimately "one." As the Heart Sutra would soon put it, "That which is Emptiness is not other than Form, that which is Form is not other than Emptiness." In other words, that which is nirvana is not other than samsara, that which is samsara is not other than nirvana.

This really changed everything. Heaven (nirvana) was no longer a state that was totally beyond this Earth (samsara). Heaven, or Spirit, was still totally transcendent to this finite relative world, but it was also completely *immanent* in it. Infinite Spirit both transcended and fully included the relative universe—they were nondual. For Buddhism, this meant the ideal was no longer the Arhat, who disappeared into nirvana while the realm of samsara and all its sentient beings burned to ashes. The new ideal was now the Bodhisattva, who promised not to disappear into nirvana but to find that prior Wholeness that allowed nirvana to be fully realized while the world of samsara was also fully arising, and what's more, to therefore be able to help all sentient beings in samsara find their own Enlightenment. All subsequent schools of Buddhism and especially those of Tantra fully accepted Nagarjuna's shunyata doctrine (it became, as T. Murti's book title has it, *The Central Philosophy of Buddhism*. Most of the truly influential spiritual schools around the world would eventually adopt some version of a nondual position).

And this meant the Two Truths were nondual as well. It was still necessary to have a satori or moksha Realization in order to know ultimate Truth; but relative truth could no longer simply be tossed in the garbage can. The entire manifest universe was a direct manifestation of Spirit itself, and was to be celebrated as the radiant luminosity of a radical Emptiness or pure Spirit. The relative world is now illusory or truly unreal *if and only if* it is perceived apart from Spirit; but when seen as it is in reality—namely, a direct manifestation of Spirit itself—then it is indeed a perfect expression of ultimate Reality.

Satori still showed a person nothing but the ultimate Truth component of nondual Reality—it was fully one with, but it did not disclose a single bit of, relative truth and the relative world. Relative truths had to be uncovered using the methods and techniques of the relative realm itself (from telescopes to microscopes to X-ray chambers to photographic plates to empirical tests in general). And this is where Guru Yoga (and the Paths of Liberation in general) started to get into real trouble. The guru was assumed to be infallible, and yet actually that was only the case when it came to ultimate Truth—it was categorically false when it came to relative truth. And that might have been fine when the relative realm in its entirety was thought to be nothing but a useless illusion; it's a completely different story when the relative reality is not-two with ultimate Reality.

This is a problem that actually affected every spiritual system in existence, although it was especially noticeable with Guru Yoga. When it comes to ultimate Truth, most of them are fairly well grounded; when it comes to relative truth, they are all on very thin ice.

And this is exactly the area that satori or Waking Up couldn't help them out with one bit. But over the next 1,000 to 2,000 years, things were learned in the relative realm about the human psyche that are of staggering importance, especially for those on a path of Waking Up. The most crucial of these facts were discovered only one hundred or two hundred years ago, yet they alter to the core how Waking Up is understood—and so far, not a single spiritual system anywhere in the world is aware of these stunning facts. This ignorance includes Guru Yoga; and this massive ignorance is exactly responsible for the problems that Guru Yoga today tends to get into such as sexual abuse and cultism—as we will clearly examine below....

So what we have at this point historically is that, in ways that matter, the guru is no longer infallible, no longer "always right." Previously, what the guru didn't know in the relative realm was not a matter of concern. It was the massive growth in relative truths (which could no longer dualistically be denied in their entirety), which especially began to pour out of humanity with the rise of modernity and the Western Enlightenment, which increasingly made what the guru didn't know in the relative realm become a real problem. Previously, what the guru didn't know in the relative realm seemed largely inconsequential since the realm itself was considered illusory. But now, what the guru doesn't know in the relative realm could kill you—more or less literally. This was always the case, of course, but the point is that, with ongoing evolution, humanity was beginning to realize just this fact. With the rise of modern science, all of the "relative truths" surrounding religion began to actually be tested using relative science—which is exactly, as we've seen, the area in which religious and spiritual "facts" do not hold up well—as the modern and postmodern world thoroughly discovered.

One way to better understand "what the guru didn't know in the relative realm" and how it would eventually severely impact guru Yoga itself—and, at the same time, to understand the types of relative truth that Guru Yoga simply *must include* if it is to become viable again—is to look at how Max Weber, the brilliant sociological philosopher, characterized the rise of modernity itself.

Weber maintained that what defined modernity specifically (meaning the era beginning with the Western Enlightenment and its discovery of virtually all the modern sciences—physics, chemistry, biology, geology, astronomy and so on) was the "differentiation of the value spheres." Before modernity, the value spheres were not yet fully differentiated, and thus their truths tended to be fused and confused. The "value spheres" specifically means the realms of the Good, the True and the Beautiful. The "Good" refers to the realm of ethics or morals (the ways that we are good to, or ethical with, each other); the "True" refers especially to objective truth, the realm of empirical science; and the "Beautiful" refers to aesthetics, artistic taste and personal authenticity. Weber's point was that, prior to modernity, these realms were not clearly differentiated—and thus morals, science and art tended to be mushed together. For example, none of the churchmen felt that they had any need whatsoever to look through Galileo's telescope; the Bible told them exactly what they would see, and that's all they needed to know. They had collapsed scientific truth with Biblical poetry and ethics, and thus none of them—not morals, not science, not art—could proceed with their own truths and their own methods, and when they were allowed to do so (as with Galileo), we have the explosion of relative knowledge that the Western Enlightenment brought with it.

Perhaps the most important—certainly as it impacted Guru Yoga—was the discovery that occurred in the area of developmental psychology (an offshoot of the discovery of evolution). Previously, throughout history, it was understood that human beings grow and develop throughout their life spans, and do so in various stages. But these stages of development were all understood in terms of their exterior, objective characteristics—such as infancy, childhood, adolescence, young adulthood, older adulthood and elderly—those are all real stages, but they are described solely in terms of something you can see on the outside. The revolutionary discovery of developmental psychology is that there are *interior stages* of development as well, and these involve various interpretive frameworks, worldviews and value systems. There are today several dozen different models describing all of this in detail, and the examples I'll give here represent only a few of the ways that this has been done.

One version of these interior stages is that of the developmental genius Jean Gebser, a variation of his interior stages being: the archaic stage, the magic stage, the mythic stage, the rational stage, the pluralistic stage and the integral stage. Abraham Maslow empirically studied these stages in terms of motivation, and he found (with Gebser's correlative stages in parentheses): physiological needs (archaic), safety needs (magic), belongingness needs (mythic), selfesteem needs (rational), self-actualization needs (pluralistic) and selftranscendence needs (integral).

Carol Gilligan gives a simplified four-stage version of development that focuses on female moral development: the woman starts out at Gilligan's stage 1, which is called *selfish*—the woman cares only for herself so this stage is also called "egocentric" or "narcissistic." At stage 2, called *care*, the woman extends care from herself to a group, her family, her clan, her tribe, her nation, her sex, her race, hence this stage is also called "ethnocentric," and it's the source of much bigoted and prejudiced values—but this can't really be helped, because it's a real stage through which all humans grow and develop; the only "cure" for this stage is to develop to the next higher stage. Stage 3 is called not "care" but "*universal care*"—the woman now extends care from her group to all groups, to all humans, regardless of race, color, sex or creed (therefore a stage also called "worldcentric," which starts to care about *universal* justice, justice for all people, not only my own group or my own race or my own religion). And stage 4, which Gilligan called "*integrated*," manages to integrate all previous stages as well as the masculine and feminine form of moral thinking (a stage also called "integral").

All of these various models are talking about the same essential levels of development or evolutionary unfolding, so they all correlate quite well with each other. Thus, the archaic/physiological and the magic/safety are both *egocentric*; the mythic/belongingness are *ethnocentric*; the rational/self-esteem and the pluralistic/self-actualization are both *worldcentric*; and the integrated/self-transcendence is *integral*. The points we will be making can all be done by using the simple stages of egocentric, ethnocentric, worldcentric and integral.

The net result of all these studies is that today there are said to be upwards of perhaps a dozen multiple intelligences—in addition to cognitive intelligence there is also emotional intelligence, moral intelligence, aesthetic intelligence, intrapersonal intelligence, motivational intelligence, values intelligence and spiritual intelligence. And as importantly different as all these intelligences or multiple *lines* of development are, they all grow and develop through around the same six to eight major *levels* of development. Some of these models have been tested in over forty different cultures—including Amazon rainforest tribes, Australian aborigines, Indianapolis housewives and Harvard professors—and no major exceptions to these stages have been found. They're truly a type of periodic table of the elements of the human mind—they are a profound and incredibly important discovery, rarely matched in all of human history.

But there are several crucial items about those stages that need to be remembered—and then we'll see exactly how profoundly they impact the realities of Waking Up and the guru's actual transmission. *Genuinely significant is that none of these stages can be seen by introspecting or looking within.* They are much more like the rules of grammar. Everybody brought up in a particular culture ends up speaking that culture's language fairly correctly—they put subject and verb together correctly, they use adjectives and adverbs correctly, and in most ways they follow that language's rules of grammar quite accurately. But ask any of them to write down what those rules are, and virtually none of them can do it. In other words, they are following a large system of complex rules quite correctly, but they have no idea they are doing so.

These interior stages of development are just like grammar—when individuals are at a particular developmental stage, they will follow the rules of that stage quite faithfully but have absolutely no idea they are doing so. And no amount of looking within, introspecting, meditating or contemplating will tell you what those stages look like. This makes these stages very difficult to discover, and that's why humanity didn't do so until only a hundred years or so ago, quite unlike Awakening or Enlightenment, which is many thousands of years old. These developmental stages of Growing Up, in other words, are very different from the states of Waking Up. One of their biggest differences is that Growing Up refers to the developmental stages that the relative self undergoes in the relative world, and Waking Up refers to the states of awareness that involve a genuine Waking Up—the former refer to relative truth, the latter refer to ultimate Truth. Another difference is that only one of them (Waking Up) can be seen by looking within or meditating. But for that reason, it is an alarming fact that, *as a rule, the Great Wisdom Traditions seem to lack awareness or understanding of the basic stages of Growing Up* because the Waking-Up traditions were laid down before these Growing-Up stages were discovered.

This is disastrous for the world's spiritual systems and for the world's Great Religions. Because one thing research has demonstrated is that these two pathways—Waking Up and Growing Up—*are* relatively *independent of each other*. You can be highly advanced in Growing Up, living at its highest developmental stages to date (worldcentric or integral), and yet still not have had a single satori realization in your entire life. And just as disturbing, you can have had a profound Waking-Up experience and yet still be at very low stages of Growing Up (such as ethnocentric). In fact, many of the world's great mystics—widely considered to be at the some of the very highest reaches of Waking Up—were nonetheless at ethnocentric stages of Growing Up, and thus they have obvious sexist, racist, homophobic, xenophobic attitudes—and worse, because their Tradition gave them no way to see and understand the stages of Growing Up (including the stage that they themselves were at), they had no way to see this inadequacy at all.

Significantly, the Great Traditions themselves were at their own lower stages of Growing Up when they were first laid down. Most of them, at their peak, were deeply ensconced at their own ethnocentric stages of Growing Up, and this is reflected in the universal existence of racist and sexist (and other ethnocentric) traits *in all of them*. Racism in the form of slavery was rampant in the Great Religions, and not a single major religion had any effective objections. Christian and

Buddhist monasteries had slaves; St. Paul counsels slaves to "obey your master and love Jesus Christ"; slavery was so widespread in earlier times that even the Native American Indians took their slaves with them on the Trail of Tears. It wasn't until the Western Enlightenment that a stage of Growing Up (the "worldcentric" or "universal care" stage) emerged that saw slavery as truly evil and, more importantly, actually did something about it. The Western Enlightenment, in Growing-Up terms, marked the first major collective emergence of the worldcentric stages from the previous ethnocentric stages, an emergence that also brought with it the rise of rationality to replace mythicliteral modes of cognition—which therefore saw the rise of the modern rational sciences of physics, chemistry, biology, geology, as well as changes in theological understanding.

The worldcentric stage—which is Gebser's "rational" stage and Gilligan's "universal care"—didn't treat one group as superior or better than another (including those who were "saved" versus those who were "damned"), but attempted to treat all humans fairly regardless of race, color, sex or creed. Where the major Great Religions had introduced powerful pockets of Waking Up, Waking Up in itself is independent of Growing Up, and thus having a Waking-Up experience was not enough to make the Great Religions condemn and remove slavery. But the emergence of the worldcentric stage (in the relative realm) during the Western Enlightenment was a higher stage of Growing Up that strenuously objected to slavery (although notice, the Western Enlightenment was not marked by any increase in Waking Up—in fact, Waking Up tended to drop off considerably, which is also another story in itself, and one that helped downgrade the trust in Guru Yoga and virtually any other system of spiritual Awakening—again, Waking Up and Growing Up are two *very* different things). But viewing slavery as deeply immoral, the worldcentric modern stage, during a roughly hundred-year period from 1770 to 1870, outlawed slavery *in every single rational-industrial country on the planet*—the first time anything like that had ever happened in humankind's entire history (despite the emergence of all sorts of Waking-Up experiences that had occurred).

The ethnocentric-laced origins of the Great Religions also show a great deal of sexism, aka the patriarchy. This lingers to this day in many of them, even those practicing genuine forms of Waking Up. One Theravada Buddhist teacher, respected for a deep degree of Enlightenment, was asked if Buddhism was sexist, and he replied, "Not at all. After all, a woman can always be reborn as a man."

The point is that indeed Growing Up and Waking Up are two deeply independent pathways, which cover respectively relative truth and ultimate Truth (but both of which are now categorically important due to nonduality). Growing Up traces the developmental process as it moves through the relative realm of the conventional and relative self, with each stage becoming more and more relatively whole, more conscious, more inclusive and more capable of positive emotions. Waking Up, on the other hand, traces the developmental process as it moves toward ultimate Truth, or the discovery of the True Self and Supreme Identity with Awakening or Self-Realization. And what research has continued to show is that those two pathways are indeed fundamentally independent—you can be at any stage of Growing Up and have a fullfledged Waking-Up or satori experience. In fact, several studies have taken well-respected spiritual teachers, known for their significant Awakening, and subjected them to standard tests measuring the growth of various multiple intelligences (in the relative realm), and overall these Awakened teachers performed no higher on all these tests than the average person did. (In other words, Waking Up does not in itself increase Growing Up.)

So you can have a Waking-Up experience at virtually any stage of Growing Up. And this is something no religion anywhere will tell you—because none of them know this truth. Every person is always experiencing some degree of both of those dimensions (from very low to very high), but the degree of achievement in each is independent of the degree in the other.

Yet a further and very important point—and this cannot be emphasized enough—is that whenever a person has a Waking-Up experience, that experience *will be interpreted according to the stage of*

Growing Up the person is at. This fact has a staggering impact on every spiritual system of Waking Up anywhere in the world.

Even if, during the actual time period that a person is experiencing a Waking Up, they are completely beyond thinking, as soon as they come out of that experience, they will start to explain it to themselves, they will use the mind to make sense of what happened—and as soon as they do that in any way, they are using the relative mind to interpret the experience, and *that relative mind in all cases is a multiple intelligence that grows and develops through the major stages of Growing Up.*

This is what makes the discovery of these Growing-Up stages so stunningly important for any sort of Waking-Up spirituality. God is an ultimate, how we think about God is a relative; and although that ultimate Realm (of Waking Up) is timeless, boundless and unchanging, that relative realm (of Growing Up) evolves over time, it develops through succinct stages of values and worldviews, each of which have massively different characteristics that have developed and evolved through time (and continue to actively evolve to this day)—and how we interpret that Waking Up depends almost entirely on our stage of Growing Up.

This was empirically demonstrated by the work of James Fowler, who studied people's spiritual interpretations, and found in virtually all cases that those grow and develop through major levels. (These are the stages or levels of the multiple intelligence known as "spiritual intelligence." Spiritual intelligence refers to how one interprets one's spiritual reality—and that interpretation, using mental terms and concepts, is a relative truth that unfolds through Growing Up in six to eight major qualitative stages. As such, spiritual intelligence is completely different from an actual spiritual experience of Waking Up in ultimate Truth. The latter is an immediate, nonverbal and nonconceptual *direct experience*; the former is a conceptual, mental, verbal *interpretation* of that experience and other spiritual realities.) Spiritual *intelligence* represents relative truth; spiritual *experience* represents ultimate Truth. And where ultimate Truth is indeed boundless, changeless, timeless, relative truth grows and evolves and develops in time through discrete stages of evolution.

So, not surprisingly, Fowler's research also found that people interpret their spiritual environment (or what they consider to be of "ultimate concern") in ways that reflect indeed the stages of Growing Up through which all multiple intelligences develop—and thus Fowler's stages are quite similar to Gebser's stages, which, as we recall, are: archaic, magic, mythic, rational, pluralistic and integral.

Thus, a Christian at the magic stage, for example, will be attracted to the New Testament because of all the magic and miracles that Christ displays—healing the sick, walking on water, curing the lame, flying through air, rising from the dead and so on. They think that if they believe with sufficient faith they will magically get that new job, get the girl, get the new car and so on—they will be magically rewarded for their faith. If Buddhist, they will repeat a mantra in order to magically get things in the relative realm for themselves (i.e., they are egocentric). At the mythic (or what Fowler called the "myth-icliteral") stage, the person will believe that every word in the Bible is literally true and is the absolute and unerring word of God, and that the Bible represents the one and only true religion in the entire world, with all other believers bound for eternal hell—this is a shift upward from an egocentric stage to an ethnocentric stage: not just me, but my special group, is saved for all eternity (while everybody else is still damned to hell). Somebody at the next higher stage, the rational (or beginning worldcentric) stage, will be attracted to all the moral (and very rational) principles in the New Testament, including the Sermon on the Mount. Or, at this rational stage, they might rationally look at all of it and decide none of it makes any sense and become an atheist. It is important to note that an atheist who decides to be an atheist for rational reasons is still at this stage of rational spiritual intelligence. A pluralistic-stage believer will not be as strictly rational but will be more "relativistic" and "multicultural"—seeing Christ as one authentic world teacher among many other authentic world teachers—after all, who are we to judge that somebody is better? (This standard postmodern "anti-judgmental" and "egalitarian" value flourishes at this stage.) They will be attracted to all of the "deconstructive" aspects of Christ's teachings, such as the weak inheriting the world (a fine example of "inverting hierarchies"), and they will particularly try to express the *social justice* they see in Christ's teachings (and Buddhists at this stage are actually called "social Buddhists" or "social-justice Buddhists"). Notice that both the rational and the pluralistic stages are "world-centric," as they have moved from an ethnocentric stage that believes Christianity and only Christianity can provide a real salvation (with everybody else being totally damned) to a stage of *universal care* where all humans—regardless of race, color, sex or religious creed—have equal access to genuine liberation. An integral-stage approach is aware of all of those perspectives and takes all of them into account, realizing that people at different stages will necessarily see and interpret the world—and Spirit—quite differently.

The point is that there wasn't just one Sermon on the Mount—there were six of them. Each person at a different stage actually heard a truly different message, and they couldn't help but do so given the unavoidable nature of the mind's development—and thus all of those stages are real, although each higher stage is, in a sense, "more real." As Hegel put it, each stage is adequate, each higher stage is more adequate. But the point is, they are all dramatically different—and this changes everything.

The same applies with full force to the whole notion of transmission. We'll return later to the idea of transmission, but for right now, simply note that a student can receive a transmission of spiritual energy—which is said to be the subtle energy that corresponds with an Awakened awareness, and an energy that the guru, it is claimed, can transmit directly to the student, facilitating a Waking Up of the same Awakened awareness in the student—but if that is so, notice that this transmission has no effect on the stage of Growing Up the student is at. If the student is at egocentric or ethnocentric or world-centric or integral stages of development before transmission, they will be at exactly the same stage after transmission. This can even be a damaging and dangerous situation, because the fact that the Waking-Up traditions have little understanding of the Growing-Up stages means that a guru can transmit a spiritual Awakening energy to a student at even the lowest stages of Growing Up—at egocentric or ethnocentric stages—and what that will do is energize those stages without fundamentally changing them. The result is then, for example, a strongly ethnocentric mystical state that truly thinks its prejudices and bigotries are coming straight from God and are totally endorsed by absolute Spirit. Historical texts make very clear, for instance, that many of the Crusaders—both Christian and Muslim alike—had very profound mystical Waking-Up experiences, and—because those deep spiritual experiences were interpreted by ethnocentric stages of Growing Up—they were simply convinced that their Tradition, and their Tradition alone, had the one and only true God, and the other side was nothing but infidels, heathens and apostates, who, if they could not be converted, were only to be tortured and summarily murdered. It's no accident that many of Hitler's inner circle (e.g., Himmler) were deeply interested in Waking-Up practices and esoteric blood-and-soil mysticism. And it's no accident that many cultic movements today typically involve a mystical Waking-Up core experience surrounded by many numerous, relative, ethnocentric beliefs about their own unique superiority and their sole capacity to deliver ultimate Truth.

In fact, what we call a "cult" is exactly a group organized at the ethnocentric stages of its own Growing Up, where a single special group is thought to be superior to all others, and the leader of that group is given an utterly supreme status. The status of the cult leader is especially disturbing, because they are invariably taken to be God (or extremely Godlike), and yet this doesn't mean just in ultimate Truth, where all beings are equally one with God, but is also taken to be true in relative truth, which simply elevates their finite personhood to an infinitely exalted status and makes "the guru can do no wrong" a deeply problematic falsehood (and in worse cases, it leads directly to things like the Jonestown Massacre in 1978, in which over 900 members of the People's Temple cult, led by their god-king Jim Jones, died in a mass suicide-murder by drinking cyanide-laced Kool-Aid).

What all of this means is that if a person goes to a guru and begins study, that guru might be quite Enlightened or have had a profound Waking Up, but at the same time they might also be at virtually any stage of Growing Up. The profound problem here is that, if the guru is believed to "never be wrong," and yet they are operating from a low level of Growing Up, the students are going to be forced to accept for ultimate reality items that are in fact deep pathologies. The major point here is simply that gone are the days where a genuine Waking Up was all that you needed in order to be authentically and fully self-realized. Waking Up itself is no longer nearly enough. Yet most of the authority of the guru—and especially the whole issue of "infallibility"—rests deeply on the idea that Waking Up itself is indeed enough. When the guru has an Enlightenment or Waking-Up experience that you don't, and you choose to turn your autonomy over to the guru in order to get this Waking Up, you are giving the guru control over the areas of your life that include those that the guru knows absolutely nothing about and, indeed, may actually be pathologically or dysfunctionally adapted to themselves. The genuine disaster here is that you get not only the Enlightened part of the guru, you get the guru's sickness as well—and you can't tell the difference.

Part of the dignity of modernity and the differentiation of the value spheres is that we have discovered much about these pathways of relative development—we know what they are and how to accelerate them. Combining that information with the traditional knowledge of Waking Up gives us an unprecedented chance to create a truly integrated (Integral) approach to spiritual understanding, an approach that includes but transcends Traditional systems.

It's time that we treat gurus exactly the same way that we treat physics professors. Instead of having an infallible view about everything of importance, they have a truly reliable view only about the techniques, practices, methods and means to help individuals Wake Up to their own True Self and Supreme Identity. When it comes to relative reality and the relative world, those truths have to be discovered on their own—they can no longer be dismissed as part of the totally illusory world.

One item that a guru has traditionally been known for—that of transmitting a subtle energy to their students that accelerates the process of Waking Up—is still a capacity with which gurus can be expected to help, in my opinion. This transmission process is not as far out as it sounds. Human beings in general are always transmitting their fundamental energetic state. If you are around somebody who is joyously happy, you tend to feel that happiness, too. If they are radiating a deep peace, you'll tend to feel that. Likewise, if you are around somebody who is profoundly depressed, you will tend to feel sad as well. As you grow and develop in the path of Waking Up, and you attain higher and higher states of consciousness, you will to some degree transmit those states, and the people around you will notice them. Many schools of Guru Yoga actually have practices where you can learn to intensify this transmission effect and control it to a significant degree. Known by names such as *shaktipat* ("the transmission of shakti or subtle energy"), gurus are often known for the power of shaktipat that they demonstrate. Whatever we decide about that, it is something that I believe is real and would remain in the basket of things the guru can legitimately engage in—along with the already acknowledged other practices and exercises that can help students progress along the path of Waking Up.

As for the appropriate attitude to take toward the guru, if you have chosen that person to be your spiritual teacher, the appropriate attitude is no longer a special and unique ontological status but simply a functional status. That is, it's no longer appropriate to look at a guru as being some sort of unique, exceptional, elevated being who alone knows all the answers and who alone is God. When it comes to relaxing the egoic self-contraction into a oneness with the entire Ground of Being, it is entirely appropriate to look at the guru as being a perfect manifestation of that ultimate Reality, as somebody who is deeply God-realized (assuming, of course, that in your opinion they indeed have had a genuine Waking Up, and this is why you have chosen them). But this is not an ontological status possessed by this guru alone; it is the ontological status of every sentient being in existence. But you can (and should) elevate the guru to an exalted status in a special way, although only on a *functional* basis. That is, the guru is indeed infinitely beyond your own present status; but the guru is representing a status that your own True Self fully possesses, and you will see the guru as specially possessing this status only until you realize your own, whereupon the guru returns to his or her actual status: an acknowledged honor of being one who has realized the ultimate Reality of their own being, which is a Reality possessed by all beings but realized by few—and that in itself deserves enormous respect, exactly the same amount your own realization of this Reality deserves.

ABOUT THE TEACHERS AND STUDENTS REFERENCED IN THIS BOOK

MARY ADAMS, born in 1953, studied South Asian philosophy and then traveled and lived for several years in India, studying under such masters as Sri Nisargadata Maharaj. She eventually moved to England and became a practicing psychotherapist. She met Andrew Cohen in 1987 and was one of his closest students until the dissolution of Andrew's organization, EnlightenNext, in 2013. She is the co-founder of the intercivilizational dialogue project 3rd Space, and is writing a book on post-patriarchal leadership.

PETER BAMPTON is a British-born (1965) spiritual teacher and co-founder, with his wife Cynthia, of the Awakened Life Project in Portugal. His main teacher was Andrew Cohen.

CHARLOTTE JOKO BECK (1917-2011) was an American Zen teacher, founder of the Ordinary Mind Zen School and author. Her teacher was Maezumi Roshi and her Dharma heirs include Barry Magid.

SANIEL BONDER, born in 1950 in New York City, is a former disciple of Adi Da and is the founder of the Waking Down. With his wife, Linda Groves, he co-founded the Human Sun Institute. Together, they teach Waking Down and Waking Down in Mutuality.

STEVE BRETT was born in 1952 in the U.K. and spent several years in India, studying with Buddhist teachers, before meeting Andrew Cohen in 1987. He was one of Andrew Cohen's closest students until the dissolution of Andrew's organization, EnlightenNext, in 2013. Today, Steve is an independent scholar and the co-founder of the intercivilizational dialogue project 3rd Space.

MARIANA CAPLAN, born in 1969, is a psychotherapist, yoga teacher and author in the fields of psychology and spirituality. As a psychotherapist, she has helped spiritual practitioners and teachers of all traditions and worked with complex traumas within spiritual communities; as a yoga teacher, she founded and teaches the Yoga & Psyche Method. Her primary teacher was Lee Lozowick.

SWAMI CHINMAYANANDA (1916-1993) was a Hindu teacher of Advaita Vedanta and a native of India. He founded the international Chinmaya Mission nonprofit spiritual-educational organization, authored nearly a hundred publications and taught Indian philosophy in universities worldwide. He was a disciple of Swami Sivananda and a teacher of James Swartz.

ANDREW COHEN, born in 1955 in New York City, was a disciple of H.W.L. Poonja and became a spiritual teacher in 1986. He created the teaching of Evolutionary Enlightenment, founded the nonprofit organization EnlightenNext and launched *EnlightenNext* magazine. The organization collapsed in 2013, when Andrew was convinced by his senior students to resign from his teaching position. But as early as 2004, with the publications of *Enlightenment Blues* and the blog *What Enlightenment!?*, allegations of abuse of power and money surfaced. After two years in retreat, he began teaching again and leading retreats. His past students include the author of this book as well as Peter Bampton, Mary Adams, Steve Brett and Thomas Steininger.

ADI DA (1939-2008), born Franklin Jones (aka Bubba Free John, Da Free John and other names), was an American spiritual teacher, writer and artist. He was a disciple of Swami Muktananda and began teaching in the early 1970s in California. He spent the last twenty-five years of his life with a small group of devotees on a Fijian island. However, in the mid-1980s, allegations surfaced by several of his former followers of sexual abuse, assault and involuntary servitude, which attracted media attention from around the world. He was the teacher of Carolyn Lee, Saniel Bonder and Terry Patten, as well as a source of inspiration for Ken Wilber.

BILL EPPERLY, born in 1961 in New Jersey, is an integral coach, a mindfulness teacher at DePaul University and a mentor in the organization Trillium Awakening. He lives in Chicago. His teachers include Brother David Steindl-Rast, Father Thomas Keating, Terry Patten and Ken Wilber.

JAMES FINLEY was born in 1943 in Ohio and currently resides in California. He is a retreat leader, Thomas Merton scholar, clinical psychologist and master of the Contemplative Way. Formerly, as a Trappist monk, he lived at the Abbey of Gethsemane in Kentucky, with Thomas Merton as his spiritual director.

STEPHEN FULDER was born in 1946 in London and earned a Ph.D. in molecular biology. He became involved in Vipassana meditation and practice in 1975, spending years in India and later moving to Israel, where he founded Tovana, the Israel Insight Society. He has been teaching Buddhist meditation practice for nearly thirty years.

ALIYA HAERI, born in 1947 in Hawaii, is a transpersonal psychologist, life coach and spiritual counselor with thirty years of international experience in psychotherapy. She is the director of the Academy of Self Knowledge (ASK) in South Africa and the wife and disciple of the Sufi teacher Shaykh Fadhlalla Haeri.

SHAYKH FADHLALLA HAERI, born in 1937 in Iraq, is a Sufi Master and spiritual philosopher, and the descendant of several generations of spiritual leaders. He lives in South Africa, where he founded the Academy of Self Knowledge (ASK), which is directed by his wife, the transpersonal psychologist and spiritual counselor Aliya Haeri. He is the author of more than thirty books on the principles of Islam, Sufism and enlightenment.

DIANE HAMILTON, born in 1958, is a mediator, group facilitator and teacher of Integral Spirituality and Zen, as well as the co-founder, with her husband, Zen teacher and lawyer Michael Mugaku Zimmerman, of Two Arrows Zen, a center for Zen study and practice with two locations in Utah. She is a Dharma heir of Genpo Roshi.

LAKSHMI, born Shanna Paice in 1980, is a disciple of Mooji and his personal assistant. She lives at Mooji's ashram, Monte Sahaja, in southern Portugal. Her initial encounter with Mooji took place at a satsang in Brixton, London, in 2007; since then, she has accompanied him on all of his tours and is instrumental in shaping the ashram's life.

CAROLYN LEE, an Australian native, is a former senior lecturer in music in the National University of Ireland, which is where she met Adi Da in 1985 and became his devotee. She has been publishing Adi Da's teachings and chronicling his life and work in her own books ever since.

LEE LOZOWICK (1943-2010) was an American teacher in the Baul spiritual tradition as well as an author, poet and blues-rock singer. He was a disciple of the Indian mystic Yogi Ramsuratrumar and was influenced by Chogyam Trungpa and G.I. Gurdjieff. He founded and led the Hohm Community in Arizona; his disciples included Mariana Caplan.

BARRY MAGID, born in 1949, is a Zen teacher, psychiatrist and psychoanalyst committed to the integration of psychodynamic psychotherapy and Zen. He founded and teaches at the Ordinary Mind Zendo in New York City. He is a Dharma heir of Charlotte Joko Beck, and his own Dharma heirs include Claire Slemmer.

THOMAS MERTON (1915-1968) was an American Trappist monk of the Abbey of Gethsemane, Kentucky; a theologian and mystic; and a writer, poet and social activist. He also studied Eastern religions, especially Zen, throughout his life. Widely recognized as an important twentieth-century Catholic mystic and thinker, he was the spiritual director of James Finley.

MOOJI, born Anthony Paul Moo-Young in 1954 in Jamaica, is an Advaita Zen Master who teaches self-inquiry and nonduality. He lives with a large group of his students at his ashram, Monte Sahaja, in southern Portugal. His teacher was H.W.L. Poonja, and Lakshmi is one of his students.

TERRY PATTEN, born in 1960, is an American integral philosopher-activist, spiritual teacher, author, coach and consultant, founder of Integral Spiritual Practice and the founder and host of the podcast *Beyond Awakening: The Future of Spiritual Practice*. With Ken Wilber and a core team, he co-authored the book *Integral Life Practice: A 21st-Century Blueprint for Physical Health, Emotional Balance, Mental Clarity, and Spiritual Awakening*. He spent fifteen years as a student of Adi Da.

H.W.L. POONJA (1910-1997), aka Papaji and Poonjaji, was a Punjabi-born Advaita teacher who lived and taught in Lucknow, India, during the later half of his life. He was a disciple of Sri Ramana Maharshi, and his own students included Andrew Cohen and Mooji.

BULENT RAUF (1911-1987) was a Turkish-British mystic and Sufi teacher who was the first president of the Muhyiddin Ibn Arabi Society, which he led until his death, and the founder of the Beshara School for Esoteric Education in Scotland. His successor is Peter (Hakim) Young.

GENPO MERZEL ROSHI, born Dennis Merzel in 1944, is an American Zen teacher who founded Kanzeon Zen Center and the Big Mind Process. Numerous allegations of sexual relationships with female students forced him to disrobe as a Buddhist monk in 2011, but he has since returned to teaching. He is a Dharma heir of Maezumi Roshi, and his Dharma heirs include Diane Musho Hamilton.

CLAIRE SLEMMER, born in 1948, is an American presentation coach, voiceover artist and semi-retired actor who has been practicing Zen for twenty years. She has been a student of Barry Magid since 2004, and is one of his Dharma heirs. She is currently the director of the Ordinary Mind Zendo in New York City.

THOMAS STEININGER, born in 1962 in Austria, is a philosopher and cultural activist, the publisher of the German magazine *Evolve*, a speaker on cultural evolution, a faculty member of Meridian University in California and the co-founder of the Emerge Dialogue Process. He was one of Andrew Cohen's closest students until the dissolution of Andrew's organization, EnlightenNext, in 2013.

JAMES SWARTZ was born in 1941 in Butte, Montana. After graduating from the University of California and moving to Waikiki, Hawaii, to start a business, he began his spiritual quest at age twenty-six, when he experienced what he calls a "life-changing epiphany" at the local Post Office, which he recounts in his book *Mystic By Default*, led him to study with Swami Chinmayananda. Today, he and his wife Sundari teach traditional Vedanta around the world, and he has written two books on the subject.

CHRISTOPHER TITMUSS was born (1944) in the U.K. and spent several years as a Theravada Buddhist monk. He is a senior Insight Meditation and Dharma teacher in the West, and an author of books on Dharma; he resides in the U.K. and teaches worldwide.

IRINA TWEEDIE (1907-1999) was a Russian-British Sufi teacher of the Naqshbandiyya-Mujaddidiya order and author of *Daughter of Fire* and *The Chasm of Fire*. She was a disciple of Hindu-Sufi sheikh Radha Mohan Lal, and her successor is Llewellyn Vaughan-Lee.

ANDRÉ VAN DER BRAAK, born in 1963, began practicing Buddhism in 1982, and was involved with spiritual teacher Andrew Cohen from 1987 to 1998. Since 2001, he has practiced Zen. In 2004, he earned a Ph.D. in comparative philosophy with a thesis on Nietzsche and Buddhism. Since 2012, he has been professor of Buddhist Philosophy in Dialogue with Other World Views at the Vrije Universiteit in Amsterdam. In 2013, he received dharma transmission in the Chinese Chan tradition from his Dutch teacher Ton Lathouwers. André's books include *Enlightenment Blues* (2003), *Goeroes en Charisma* (2006), and *Nietzsche and Zen: Self-Overcoming Without a Self* (2011).

LLEWELLYN VAUGHAN-LEE, born in 1953, is a British Sufi mystic and the lineage successor of Irina Tweedie in the Naqshbandiyya-Mujaddidiyya Sufi Order. He is a lecturer and the author of many books on Sufism, mysticism, dream work and spirituality. Since 1991, he has lived in Northern California, where he founded the Golden Sufi Center.

KEN WILBER (1949) is an American philosopher and writer on transpersonal psychology and the creator of Integral Theory and Integral Spirituality, as well as the founder of the Integral Institute. His thinking has been influenced by the Buddhist philosophy of Nagarjuna.

PETER (HAKIM) YOUNG was born in 1949 in London. In the mid-1970s he enrolled at the Beshara School at the Chisholme Institute as a student, and served as principal of the school from 1984 to 2015, taking over the organization's direction after the death of Bulent Rauf. Since leaving Chisholme, he has been running green wood-working courses.

REFERENCES

Aivanhov, Omraam Mikhael (1982). *What Is a Spiritual Master?* Frejus, France: Editions Prosveta

Ambrose, Alice and Lazerowitz, Morris (1972). *Ludwig Wittgenstein: Philosophy and Language.* New York: Routledge

Anthony, Dick; Ecker, Bruce; and Wilber, Ken (1987). "When Is Religion Transformative? A Conversation with Jacob Needleman." From Anthony, D., Ecker, B., and Wilber, K., Editors, *Spiritual Choices: The Problem of Recognizing Authentic Paths to Inner Transformation.* New York: Paragon House Publisher

Batchelor, Stephen, and Patton, Nancy (2002). "The Twins: Faith and Doubt." *Mandala* Magazine Archives, the Foundation for the Preservation of the Mahayana Tradition (FPMT.com), September–November 2002 issue

Berzin, Alexander (2010). *Wise Teacher, Wise Student: Tibetan Approaches to a Healthy Relationship.* Ithaca, New York: Snow Lion Publications

Caplan, Mariana (2011). *The Guru Question: The Perils and Rewards of Choosing a Spiritual Teacher*, Boulder, Colorado: Sounds True Publishing

Caplan, Mariana. "Psychology and Spirituality: One Path or Two?," *The Huffington Post* (September 1, 2011)

Eisenstadt, Shmuel Noah and Buber, Martin (1992). *On Intersubjectivity and Cultural Creativity.* Chicago: University of Chicago Press

Feuerstein, Georg (1990). *Holy Madness: The Shock Tactics and Radical Teachings of Crazy-Wise Adepts, Holy Fools, and Rascal Gurus.* New York: Paragon House

Fischer, Norman (1999). "The Teacher in the West." *Lion's Roar* Magazine (September 1, 1999)

Gampopa (1998). *The Jewel Ornament of Liberation: The Wish-Fulfilling Gem Of The Noble Teachings.* Translated by Khenpo Konchog Gyaltsen Rinpoche, edited by Ani K. Trinlay Chodron. Ithaca, New York: Snow Lion Publications

Hori, G. Victor Sogen (2000). "Koan and Kensho in the Rinzai Zen Curriculum." From Steven Heine and Dale S. Wright, editors, *The Koan. Texts and Contexts in Zen Buddhism.* Oxford, U.K.: Oxford University Press

Johnston, Charles MD. (1991). *Necessary Wisdom: Meeting the Challenge of a New Cultural Maturity.* Seattle, Washington: ICD Press

Jones, Franklin (2004). *The Knee of Listening.* Middletown, California: Dawn Horse Press

Jung, Carl (1969). Foreword to Suzuki's "Introduction to Zen Buddhism." *Collected Works of C. G. Jung,* Vol. 11. 2nd edition. Princeton, New Jersey: Princeton University PressSurya Das, Lama (2009). *The Mind Is Mightier Than the Sword: Enlightening the Mind, Opening the Heart.* New York: Doubleday

Magid, Barry (2005). *Ordinary Mind: Exploring the Common Ground of Zen and Psychotherapy.* Boston: Wisdom Publications

Malcolm, Norman (1984). *Ludwig Wittgenstein: A Memoir,* with "A Biographical Sketch" by Georg Henrik von Wright. New York: Oxford University Press

Persico, Tomer (2013). *Andrew Cohen and the Decline of the Guru Institution.* Available from TomerPersicoEnglish.Wordpress.com/2013/08/13

Prem, Sri Krishna (1958). *The Yoga of the Bhagavad Gita.* Baltimore, Maryland: Penguin Books

Salzberg, Sharon. "Of Teachers and Teaching: Who Is a Teacher? What Is a Teacher?" *Insight Newsletter.* Barre, Massachusetts: Barre Center for Buddhist Studies (Fall 1993)

Scholem, Gershom (1969). *On the Kabbalah and Its Symbolism.* New York: Schoken Books

Steiner, George (2003). *Lessons of the Masters.* Cambridge, Massachusetts: Harvard University Press

Titmuss, Christopher (2015). *The Buddha of Love: Essay on the Power of the Heart*. Lulu.com: Lulu Publishing

Vaughan-Lee, Llewellyn. "What Does It Mean to Be a Teacher. StudyMode.com (January 7, 2015)

Wach, J. (German 1925, English 1962). "Master and Disciple: Two Religio-Sociological Studies." *The Journal of Religion* 42(1): 1–21

Wilber, Ken (1999). *One Taste*. Boston: Shambhala Publications

Xenophon (1994). *Memorabilia*. Translated from Greek by Amy L. Bonnette. Ithaca, New York: Cornell University Press

ABOUT THE AUTHOR

Amir Freimann was born in 1958 and grew up in a small village in Israel, becoming interested in spiritual-existential questions at the age of sixteen. He served in the Israeli army and became a pacifist after participating in the 1982 Lebanon War. He spent two years meditating in a Zen monastery in Japan, and completed five years of medical studies in Jerusalem. At that point, following a meeting with a young American spiritual teacher, Andrew Cohen, he decided to devote his life to spiritual awakening, and spent over twenty years doing intense spiritual practice and engaged in philosophical-spiritual exploration in Andrew's community, EnlightenNext, in the United States. In 2009, he left the community and moved back to Israel, with the intention of participating in and facilitating cultural-spiritual development in Israeli society. With a group of leading educators, he founded the Israeli Education Spirit Movement, of which he is the managing director, and co-edited two books about the connection between education, philosophical inquiry and spiritual seeking. Amir is married and lives in the village where he grew up, where he is working on his doctoral thesis, "Living Transcendence—A Phenomenological Study of Exemplars of Exceptional Spiritual Development."

He can be reached at amirfreimann@gmail.com or via his website, Free2Quest.com.

CPSIA information can be obtained
at www.ICGtesting.com
Printed in the USA
LVHW030829011118
595539LV00002B/2